Reclaiming Our Children, Reclaiming Our Schools

Reclaiming Our Children, Reclaiming Our Schools

Reversing Privatization and Recovering Democracy in America's Public Schools

Eric Shyman

ROWMAN & LITTLEFIELD
Lanham • Boulder • New York • London

Published by Rowman & Littlefield
A wholly owned subsidiary of The Rowman & Littlefield Publishing Group, Inc.
4501 Forbes Boulevard, Suite 200, Lanham, Maryland 20706
www.rowman.com

Unit A, Whitacre Mews, 26-34 Stannary Street, London SE11 4AB

Copyright © 2017 by Eric Shyman

British Library Cataloguing in Publication Information Available

Library of Congress Cataloging-in-Publication Data Available

ISBN 978-1-4758-2989-1 (cloth : alk. paper)
ISBN 978-1-4758-2990-7 (pbk. : alk. paper)
ISBN 978-1-4758-2991-4 (electronic)

∞™ The paper used in this publication meets the minimum requirements of American National Standard for Information Sciences—Permanence of Paper for Printed Library Materials, ANSI/NISO Z39.48-1992.

Printed in the United States of America

Contents

Preface

It is virtually impossible to be involved in education contemporarily and not have fervent opinions on its state, one way or another. Indeed, many, if not most, of these issues are seriously divisive; perhaps more divisive than they have ever been in the past. However, the discrepancy between those who experience, on a daily basis, the ramifications of the privatization of education and those who appear to be in control of its implementation is vast. While teachers have been regarded as a marginalized professional group for quite a while, the level of their marginalization has reached new depths and broadened in the past decade. Never before have teachers been so deeply vilified, chastised, and demoralized in the mass media, political commentary, and legislation than they are today, and schools are beginning to pay the ultimate price for it.

Even a cursory look at the history of education reform in American public schools reveals a system in which teachers have been relegated to being mere functionaries, there to deliver the curriculum that is imparted to them by an administration, a board of education, or, has been the case of late, a seemingly clandestine committee questionably qualified individuals who have usurped the policymaking and governmental systems to serve their own profitable ends. or, as has been the case of late, a seemingly clandestine committee of questionably qualified individuals who have usurped the policymaking and governmental systems to serve their own profitable ends. The result of this pernicious process is clear: the schooling process becomes deeply undemocratic, ableistic, elitist, segregated, and disinterested in the public's perspective, educationists' expertise, and emotional well-being of students.

It is fair to suggest that the public school is the most defining characteristic of a democratic society. In what more direct way can a people exercise its control in its own society and culture than by determining what its future learns to do, think, believe, and say? This sentiment can be traced back directly to the founding fathers who, though romanticized in many ways, undoubtedly held the process of education as the most likely antidote to tyranny and hereditary aristocracy. As a result, though beset with many problems, inequities, and inconsistencies, the American public school system was virtually preordained to be an outgrowth of the democratic experiment. But was it ever truly realized and implemented in the service of democracy?

While this argument can be approached in many ways and from multiple perspectives, one consistent fact is the deep faith that the American people have placed in the school system, however unlikely and unrealistic, to be a near complete panacea for its social ills. Indeed, I too began this writing project, which produced two separate works, with the same inclination and deep belief. That is, that whatever the social problem, cultural conflict, or political disagreement, the school would be the site of its resolution; idealistic, indeed, but something that I have always believed.

However, after immersing in depth in the research process I found, as I often do, a pathway to a very different conclusion. The conclusion is not, as may be inferred, that I no longer have the faith I did in the public school system. If anything this faith has grown deeper and stronger as a result of this project. Rather, it is the arbitrary faith we place in a system that we care for and contribute so little to that is problematic. To believe in the power of schooling and education is as democratic as one can be: that when one is permitted to think for oneself, one's conclusions are entirely independent and, with that, one has become a free thinker. I hold on to this belief tightly. However, to believe that schools, by their very existence, can ameliorate the very deep social and cultural problems that pervade American society without care, attention, and truly meaningful investment is to be outright foolish.

The issue, in many ways, distills to a matter of control. Who controls the curriculum? Who controls the laws? Who controls the assessment? Who controls the policymakers? This is the point at which the pessimism, though discomfiting, must take its realistic hold. America has effectively forged a society that is less about cultural growth than it is about financial and economic prosperity. This deeply capitalistic worship of money has been ever-present in society since at least the Industrial Revolution of the late nineteenth century, if not earlier. But the theoretical foundation of the "free market" as being a liberating force has become an outright fallacy; if it were ever true to begin with.

Instead, the growth of capitalism has led not to equality and democracy, but to economic stratification and plutocracy on a great scale in which the rich not only get richer, but the rich quite literally control the government in order to orchestrate actions in its interest. Instead of facilitating a government of a republic that was purportedly intended to be representative of the people, the role of financial prowess and its corresponding power has suffused across the governmental arena so widely and deeply that the public has become a mere relic of times past. While it is arguable that America was ever a truly practicing, functional democracy, there is little argument about whether its plutocratic nature has never reached this level before.

As the public school remains the cornerstone of a democratic society, it appears that it will also be most vulnerable when that democratic society becomes plutocratic. This is exactly what has happened in the American public school system. Through carefully crafted and deftly implemented policy changes from Reagan to Obama, and likely onward, the education system has become the newest realm of the neoliberal exploitation, transforming this precious institution from a potential epicenter of cultural, social, and political learning and action to the latest and greatest marketplace with one main, though unwitting and involuntary groups of consumers: the public.

Though history does indeed indicate that there have been times in which private interests have taken hold of public policy in the realm of schooling, these efforts remained in pockets and only tenuously sanctioned by the government; the level to which the private sector controls the public money in the area of education is unprecedented. Taking full hold with the dubious establishment and adoption of the Common Core State Standards (CCSS), its correspondingly dubious committees and councils, and the resulting surge in profiteering and lobbying opportunity for a number of well-connected and influential corporations like Pearson, Inc. and McGraw-Hill, as well as corporate-style and politically influential "not-for-profits" such as The College Board, Achieve, Inc., and the Educational Testing Service among others, the infiltration of the private sector in public schools has reached a critical mass.

Despite its apparent success, it is quite clear that both the government and the private sector underestimated the savvy perceptions of the general public. By cloaking these growing corporate influences in competitive grants such as Race to the Top, as well as punitive practices for failing to increase student achievement, the alliance between the government and the private sector relied on their perception of the obtuseness of the general public. However, it did not work. If there is one thing the public is unwilling to sacrifice, it is our children.

I write this book keeping in mind a number of vantage points. First and foremost, I write it as a citizen who is fulfilling my civic duty in standing up for what I believe in and acting in the face of countless violations of social justice. Second, I write this book as a father of two children, one of whom is currently attending public school, and the other who will be doing so in due time. I intend to send my children to public school for their entire K-12 schooling career, and believe that, as a result, my voice (as well as their voices, when they find them) must be heard. There is nothing a parent will not do to fight for justice for their children, and I join the ranks of parents past who have been doing the same for quite some time. Third, I write this book as an educationist: a teacher, professor, educational philosopher, researcher, and writer, and one whose voice will not be silenced despite any concerted effort to do so.

But finally, I write this book as an American who believes that being American also means deeply valuing those who are not American, were not always American, do not want to be American, or are not even aware of what being American may mean. Indeed a statement such as this can be easily misconstrued, misinterpreted, or seen as maligning America and being American. However, it is not; quite the opposite, in fact, is true. I realize America, and the depth of being American, is to fully realize that what the founding fathers *said* America is about and what America has become is disjointed. Indeed, there has been equality, but only for some, which remains inequality. Indeed there has been justice, but only for some, which remains injustice. It is a sad but deep truth that America has never been for all, but only for some.

It is this point at which I recapitulate my faith in schooling. I believe deeply in schools' ability to change society, to create children with deep, just, civic obligations who become citizens of America as well as the world. But we can only fulfill this role of the schools if we invest in the right way. This does not mean allowing private corporations to infiltrate our public system for their own profit, to dictate what it means to be educated, what it means to achieve, what it means to be up to a standard of its own choosing. That is not up to them, it is up to us: the public. The time has come that we must separate ourselves from the vocal and powerful minority who seek to overtake what is rightfully ours.

This sense of unity is not to say that the public must agree on all issues, to come up with a uniform curriculum, to come to a consensus on what all children should know, think, and do. Quite the opposite is true: the spirit and function of a truly democratic school system is one which is able to traverse its differences, incorporate its disagreements, and translate such discourse into a pluralistic, academically free, and thoughtful process which produces global citizens with a deep sense of civic duty, not responders or workers who fulfill an economic function.

This book is written in the hopes of being a contribution, and an intentionally provocative one, to the conversation regarding the private takeover of the public schools. To be sure, it is a polemic intended to vehemently refute, rebuke, and reject the role that the private sector has come to play in public schooling through a number of initiatives. Conversely, it is a polemic that argues for the public, the *true* public, to reclaim our schools, reclaim our democracy, reclaim our freedom, and reclaim our children.

Introduction

Reclaiming Our Children, Reclaiming Our Schools: Reversing Privatization and Recovering Democracy in America's Public Schools is not only a call to thinking and discussion, but also a call to action; one that is intended to be heard by anyone who truly cares about the future of our children and society at a global level. Over the past three decades the American public school system has been the site of a crafty, stealthy, and barely perceptible usurpation by the corporate elite and private sector, and the critical mass has indeed been reached. While the rhetoric behind these efforts remain cloaked in populist and democratic terms such as school choice, civil rights, and achievement gaps, as well as nationalistic connotations such as global competitiveness, economic well-being, and even national security we, as the public, must not be fooled. There is one ends to the current education reform effort and one ends only: profiteering.

As the distance between public participation in governmental processes and actual legislative and political efforts narrows drastically, the one area that the public was always believed to maintain, the public schools, has become the final and bloodiest victim to the solidifying plutocracy in America. Whether the schools ever truly belonged in the public's control is, indeed, arguable. However, even in its turbulence, teachers and children, who are the true experts and receptors of this expertise, were generally given the room and freedom to address their needs as somewhat autonomous local contingents.

Over the past 10 years, however, the clandestine setting up of the ultimate neoliberal takeover of our schools has come to a head, and the public school system has been unmistakably usurped by the profit-based interests of the private sector, and they have been allowed entrance directly by the government. The sacred space of schooling has now fallen prey to the unscrupulous control of the corporate elite, and the public has become their unwitting consumers, with the children paying the highest price for their profits.

It would be foolish to deny that there are deep problems that are entrenched in the public school system in America, with some neighborhoods, specifically those with economic challenges which remain largely inhabited by black and Hispanic people, reaping far more than their share of negative consequences. It is upon these emotional and social issues that the corporate-backed education faction capitalizes, both figuratively and literally. Undoubtedly the inhabitants of these neighborhoods want the best for their communities, children, and families, and a public system that has been designed to work against them is clearly an ineffective means of doing so. Their schools remain housed in dilapidated, unsafe, unsanitary buildings, and they are provided with old and tattered textbooks and sparse availability of materials, all of which propagates society's consistent messages of devaluation and disinterest. Society's mistrust is recapitulated every morning as the children pass through metal detectors and with ever-present police threatening legal punishment.

Moreover, the corporate movement is not entirely detached from these public issues; quite the contrary, it depends upon them. It addresses legitimate issues faced by the school system, and uses these issues to gain its ground. Indeed, money, a central issue in school functioning, is desperately needed, more in challenged minority neighborhoods than in others, and what better resource for money is there but the private sector, in which it seems to be nearly limitless and easier to access than through bureaucratic governmental processes. What is missed, however, is that these processes are no longer separate, and to buy into one system is to, by default, buy into the other. The result is clear. What essentially happens is the provision of the same disservice and poor quality of schooling, while the corporations profit handsomely from the sale of its curricular and assessment materials to the schools.

These privatization efforts are not limited to only public schooling at the K-12 level, however. Increasingly private interests are making their way into higher education via state education departments as well. The most pernicious means of doing so is by monopolizing teacher certification tests in multiple states, forcing teachers to pay hefty sums in order to fulfill requirements that, in many cases, have little connection with their teacher training or their actual mode of teaching content. Furthermore, in a number of states, an additional requirement known as Teacher Performance Assessment (edTPA), a portfoliobased teacher candidate assessment stemming from the California Teacher Performance Assessment, is required in addition to certification examinations. All of these tests are published and sold by private companies, with Pearson, Inc. being the most commonly used. In total, teacher candidates in many states are forced to spend upwards of $2–3,000 of additional costs simply to acquire the bare minimum requirements for state certification.

The purpose of the book is not to relay or perpetuate a pessimistic message, however. Quite contrarily, there is much hope to be garnered, with genuine success that can only be achieved without the mercenary meddling of the private sector. While the American school system is, indeed, in a state of disarray, and has been for some time, it has become more so by the current neoliberal efforts purported to "save it." That is, the corporatization, while presented as the promise of a reform never quite realized in past efforts, has not only left the same broken system in its place, but has actually exacerbated the situation. Children in struggling neighborhoods continue to be underserved, undereducated, and devalued, even as they are more severely segregated, disciplined, and dealt with.

This book will examine deeply how the public school system was quite literally put up for sale to the private sector by our very own government. Beginning with a brief history of education reform in America, it will be revealed that the public school system was never truly set up for democratic ends, at least in the way that genuine democratic thinkers such as John Dewey define it. Instead, it will be demonstrated that American schools were largely set up to assimilate and Americanize children, especially those from "culturally deprived" or foreign families, such as black children, Latino children, and the sons and daughters of immigrants.

This initial setup will lead to an exploration of how the corporate elite were able to gain access to the public school system through clever uses of public assistance projects, political alliances, and lobbying efforts, namely, in the area of educational testing, curricular materials, and the establishment of charter school. Through this exposition it will be demonstrated that despite the lofty promises made by the corporate-backed charter school system, such promises remained undelivered and, in fact, aggravated an already dire situation.

Finally, a number of ideas regarding how American schools can eliminate the corporate influence and change, for the better, on its own volition through public participation will be proffered. Specifically addressed will be the means of handling the issues of true local control, the central role that teachers and educationists must play in the reform process, issues in teacher preparation, power dynamics, nurturing true citizenship, investing wholly and wisely in struggling communities, and embracing and addressing the harsh realities that racism, xenophobia, classism, ableism, and sexism play. This book intends to be a step toward regaining our democracy through our public schools.

Chapter 1

How We Got Here
Education Reform in a Nutshell

The history of reform in education is almost entirely contemporaneous with the establishment of the public school system itself. The deep American belief in education and its connection to social change and utilitarian efforts has been evident from the beginning of the republic's founding. As John Adams passionately suggested:

> Laws for the liberal education of the youth, especially of the lower class of people, are so extremely wise and useful, that, to a humane and generous mind, no expense for this purpose would be thought extravagant.[1]

Further exalting the power and utter necessity of education, Adams implored:

> It should be your care, therefore, and mine to elevate the minds of our children and exalt their courage; to accelerate and animate their industry and activity; to excite in them a habitual contempt of meanness, abhorrence of injustice and humanity, and an ambition to excel in every capacity, faculty, and virtue. If we suffer their minds to grovel and creep in infancy, they will grovel all their lives.[2]

Indeed, the public school is perhaps the hallmark of a democratic society, as an educated public has always been venerated as the distinctive antidote to tyranny. As Jefferson famously quips, "An educated citizenry is a vital requisite for our survival as a free people."[3] More fervently, Jefferson declares in a letter to William C. Jarvis:

> I know of no safe depositary of the ultimate powers of the society but the people themselves; and if we think them not enlightened enough to exercise their control with a wholesome discretion, the remedy is not to take it from them, but

to inform their discretion by education. This is the true corrective of abuses of constitutional power.[4]

Though the education system at the time of the founding fathers was relegated to largely private and religious-based organizations, the value of education was quite clearly elevated to the highest degree. Despite this value, however, there was ever a tension between those Americans who believed in the regulatory power of governments and those who were wary of any form of meddling by the federal government in local affairs. Indeed, the main point of contention between the Federalists and anti-Federalists was this very issue. By the time Horace Mann began to advocate for a well-structured and truly public educational system in the 1840s, this schism was deeply engrained in the political narrative. Despite this deep wariness, however, Mann was largely successful in establishing the infrastructure for what would become the public school system.

By the late nineteenth century, there appeared to be a prominent group of educational thinkers, known in the literature as "mental disciplinarians," who advocated for a classic approach to education focusing on such subjects as Greek, Latin, mathematics, and literature. These scholars regarded the mind as a muscle (in a near literal sense) and claimed that practice in these central curricular areas were most beneficial to creating the educated child. From this perspective, the purpose of education was not, by any means, to create workers or economic contributors, but rather well-educated and cultured citizens.[5]

This classic perspective was largely maintained as the dominant approach to curriculum until it was challenged early in the twentieth century by subscribers to a school of thought that became known as the "social efficiency theorists" or "administrative progressives."[6] Theorizing within the context of the burgeoning industrialization in America, these theorists placed emphasis on the economic contribution of schooling to the American workforce. That is, that the main function of schooling is not to create the citizen, but rather to train the worker, essentially acting as the determining agent as to what professional paths students would follow. From this perspective, all activities presented in schools should have a distinct vocational purpose with a corresponding economic function.

Also endemic in the social efficiency theory perspective was the first indication of schools being viewed not as intellectual institutions, but rather as corporate-style organizations that did not need the wisdom of educational experts, but rather the organization of adequate management and corporate structure similar to that of factories. In this sense, schools were seen as production facilities, with workers as their product. Drawing largely on the theory of Frederick Winslow Taylor, whose work influenced the management styles of factories based on productivity, Edward A. Ross and John Franklin

Bobbitt suggested that the same ideas can be applied to managing the efficiency of schools. Referring to students as "platoons" and school buildings as "plants," Ross and Bobbitt's ideas became central to social efficiency practice in schooling.[7]

The influence of the social efficiency theory on both schooling and industry was unmistakable. As the theory gained popularity and application, a number of industrial commentators began to praise the new approach to education, with one, Helen Todd, even claiming that, as a result of the connection between schooling and industry, American textiles would now be able to compete in the foreign market. This was one of the first indications of the soon-to-be educational-industrial market complex.[8]

As was to be repeated cyclically throughout the development of the public school system, the social efficiency theorists were soon challenged by a developing school of thought known as humanism, which was more aptly an outgrowth of the mental disciplinarians' developing responses to the criticisms of social efficiency theorists. The humanists, while maintaining the importance of particular areas of study over others, began to de-emphasize the role that rote memory and recitation plays in schooling. Rather, they argued, the focus of schooling should be on developing the child's civic duty and citizenship, in many ways a reprise of Adams' and Jefferson's ideas.

Equally as importantly, however, was the humanists' deep rejection of sorting students by their prospective vocation in later life. Rather, humanists believed in a system of electivism, or in allowing individual students to choose their general coursework based on their own interests. By relegating such power of choice to the student, schooling was still able to serve an economic contribution, but would allow the students themselves to determine their own path rather than being assigned one based on arbitrary decision-making processes and largely classist and racist presumptions.

Providing a different form of critique to the humanists as well as the social efficiency theorists, a school of thought that came to be known as developmentalism emerged. Developmental theorists conceptualized schooling and child development in an entirely novel way. Pioneered by such thinkers as Lev Vygotsky, Jean Piaget, and its most vocal advocate G. Stanley Hall, the developmentalists suggested that predetermining all curricula for students was developmentally unsound. Rather, children should be encouraged to explore materials within their natural environment on their own volition and in creative, novel and self-guided ways. Overprescribing curricular activities would prove not only limiting intellectually, but prohibitive developmentally.

The progressives, a rather vague term applied to a group of educational scholars who were equally as critical of the capitalist tendencies of the developing American culture, as well as its undemocratic influences on education, was the next group intellectuals to gain dominance over curriculum theory in American schools. Among its most well-known members, John Dewey advocated the notion, similar to developmentalists, that children should lead the educational process, but extended the idea by suggesting that book learning of any kind was minimizing, and that project-based activities that were interdisciplinary and inductive was the most effective and appropriate way to teach children.

What became clear as the cycle of education reform continued in largely the same way throughout the next several decades of the twentieth century and into the twenty-first century was that the discrepancy was based on a single issue: the purpose of public schooling. While certain schools of thought, namely, the humanists and the progressives, maintained that the purpose of schools should be to create the citizen, other schools of thought, namely, social efficiency theorists, contended that schools were to be economically contributive, and responsible for creating the worker. Still, other schools of thought, such as the mental disciplinarians and developmentalists, focused more squarely on creating the erudite person, focusing little attention on either civic duty or economic contribution.

Indeed, endemic to all of these discussions is the role of American culture, and what it is thought to be by its members, especially those with political and social influence. While some maintain that American culture is more of an economic system,[9] with its basis in capitalism, others will argue that there is a deep sense of social responsibility in Americanism as well. Whether schools nurture one, the other, or both simultaneously remains fervently debated and contested on a number of levels and for a number of reasons. These contests played out in different ways across history, and continue to do so even today.

Perhaps the first instance of widespread distrust in the American public school system was the result of economic and cultural turbulence when the Russians "won the Space Race" in 1957. In response, a massive effort, including private donations from the Ford Foundation and the Carnegie Foundation to governmental initiatives focusing on enhancing science and math education (similar to the current focus on Science, Technology, Engineering and Mathematics, known collectively as STEM), was forwarded. This became one of the first entanglements between private capital and public school initiatives resulting from a perceived loss in educational quality.

Much of the social rhetoric surrounding the poor quality of America's schools in light of the "Space Race," as well as the increasing tensions regarding inequality between schools, especially as revealed by *Brown v. Board of Education* in 1957 and its aftermath, caused enough of a social stir to prompt President Lyndon Johnson to incorporate education as a main focus of his "Great Society," which was an already controversial and divisive political effort comparable to Roosevelt's "New Deal."

Likely the crowning achievement of this focus was the passing of the Elementary and Secondary Education Act (ESEA) in 1965, the first federal legislation implemented for public schooling. Largely a school financing action, ESEA was a legislative call for equalization between schools in poor black neighborhoods with their suburban white counterparts. Rekindling the American ideal of singular faith in education, Johnson's message was clear: education can save American society.

Regardless of the radical actions of "Great Society" programs, the pessimistic sentiment regarding America's public schools was maintained across several decades, complicated by a number of conservative presidential administrations to follow Johnson's. The issue culminated once again in the now ubiquitously nefarious invective against the public school system known as *Nation at Risk*, released under Reagan's administration in 1983. According to the report, purportedly as a result of a massive analysis of current data, America's public school system was in such decline that, should another country have waged such a system upon the United States it would well be seen as an "act of war."[10] In order to correct this downward spiral, American schools were compelled to increase their standards as well as their means of accountability.

Nation at Risk proved to be the foundational catalyst for the current quagmire in which the American public education system has become stuck. While the Reagan administration maintained its efforts toward decreasing the federal government's involvement in state-controlled entities such as schooling, his administration did allow the increasing influence of private corporations in public education, allowing an unprecedented number of private "independent" consultants to collect federal monies for their services. Reagan's permitting of private interests to become involved in public schooling led directly to President George H. W. Bush's "America 2000" campaign, under which he vowed that each state would overhaul its education system to perform as an efficient "corporate-style" institution marked by higher standards and higher achievement.[11]

Though contrasted in a number of ways, Bill Clinton, the first Democrat to hold office since Jimmy Carter in the late 1970s, maintained Bush's model for educational innovation, forwarding his agenda, similarly titled "Goals 2000," which served mainly as the catalyst for the reauthorization of ESEA in 1994 under the moniker "Improving America's Schools Act" (IASA). Though maintaining much of the original statute, the new version of the law made significant changes to the financial structure of Title I, the section of the law that determines how money for struggling schools will be distributed. For the first time, the receipt of these funds were linked directly to the accountability of student achievement, and mandated such funds to be used for educational efforts such as extended school days, weekend school, and summer programs.

While seemingly radical at face value, IASA simply maintained the same elitist perspective that guided all previous reforms: more money will help bring the black and Hispanic community to the standards of the white middle class. This perspective was to remain intact with the next administration of George W. Bush, but with seemingly unprecedented consequences. While many regard the educational legislation passed under the George W. Bush administration as "new," No Child Left Behind (NCLB) was merely a reauthorization of the ESEA and the IASA, and maintained much of the same structure. What was different, however, was the ceremonious nature of the signing of the bill into law, which represented a much needed, politically driven bipartisan display of support. Indeed, the publicity and fanfare depicting President Bush flanked by different combinations of black children were not accidental.[12,13]

Further, the notion of accountability and student achievement, as linked to the availability of federal funds was to take a drastic turn, and the deep, incestuous, and seemingly indelible entwinement between corporate interests and public education was to take its most significant hold. Accomplished by the seemingly innocuous reiteration of high standards and student achievement coupled with more directly overseen accountability processes, NCLB was the first version of the legislation since its inception in 1965 that was successful in maintaining oversight of accountability procedures, delivering financial consequences to those districts who did not achieve progress (mostly in poor black and Hispanic neighborhoods) and financial rewards to those districts that did (mostly those in middle- or upper-middle-class neighborhoods).

Again, little attention was paid to investment in whole communities, children, school structure, training, or curriculum development. Rather, schools were simply warned that they were expected to reach particular standards, and that the amount of money received and freedom from continual strict oversight was dependent on its achievements. By definition, this is a corporate-style, hierarchical model based only on productivity and accountability of outcomes, not on processes. This productivity was not to be based on the creativity of teachers, happiness of students, love of learning, civic development, or any other such prized educational value. Rather, it was based on the attainment of scores on assessments that were produced, marketed, and sold directly to schools by private corporations with deep ties to the political system.

Lest one concludes that the corporate interest in the public school system is facilitated only by conservative Republican administrations, perhaps the deepest and most pernicious events in public education occurred under the staunchly liberal Democratic Obama administration. Virtually cementing the overtaking of public schooling by corporate interests, Race to the Top, a $4.5 billion competitive educational grant was released in 2011.[14] Among a number of mandates for receiving the grant, from which states received between $500 million and nearly $1 billion, states were virtually forced to adopt corporate created and controlled initiatives, most notably the Common Core State Standards (CCSS) and its panoply of curricular and assessment materials and consultation services that were produced exclusively by politically tied corporate interests such as Pearson Inc., McGraw-Hill, Educational Testing Service, and Achieve Inc., among others.

The quagmire that the public education system is currently in is the direct result of this quite intentional and well-designed initiative by a fundamentally neoliberal market that is deeply embedded in both racist and classist practices, fueled by a deep-seated mistrust for the general public. Essentially, the public has been hijacked from its very proprietors: the *actual* public. This is an intolerable situation that, if continued, will turn our most prized institution of democracy into a mere depot for profiteering at the expense of America's most valuable resource: our children, if it has not done so already.

NOTES

1. John Adams (1776). "Thoughts on Government." Retrieved from http://www.constitution.org/jadams/thoughts.htm.

2. John Adams (1775). "Letter from John Adams to Abigail Adams." Retrieved from http://www.masshist.org/digitaladams/archive/doc?id=L17751029jathird.

3. Thomas Jefferson (n.d.). *The Papers of Thomas Jefferson: Digital Edition.* Retrieved from http://rotunda.upress.virginia.edu/founders/TSJN.html.

4. Thomas Jefferson (1820). "Letter from Thomas Jefferson to William C. Jarvis." Retrieved from http://famguardian.org/Subjects/Politics/thomasjefferson/jeff1350.htm.

5. Herbert M. Kliebard, *The Struggle for the American Curriculum.* (New York: Routledge, 2005).

6. Ibid.

7. Ibid.

8. Ibid.

9. Neil Postman, *The End of Education: Redefining the Value of School* (New York: Vintage, 1996).

10. *Nation at Risk*, Retrieved from http://www2.ed.gov/pubs/NatAtRisk/risk.html.

11. Alyson Klein, "Historic Summit Fueled Push for K-12 Standards" *Education Week,* September 23, 2014. Retrieved from http://www.edweek.org/ew/articles/2014/09/24/05summit.h34.html on September 16, 2015

12. http://abcnews.go.com/topics/news/education/no-child-left-behind.htm?mediatype=Image.

13. http://www.americanrhetoric.com/speeches/gwbushnochildleftbehindsigning.htm.

14. http://www2.ed.gov/programs/racetothetop/index.html.

Chapter 2

Be American

Assimilation and the Dominant Middle-Class Ethic in Schools

One of the most controversial issues in the American experiment is the nature of American culture: how it is defined, characterized, and transmitted, as well as who must become a part of it. The role that public schools play in this discussion is central as, from the very beginning of its formal establishment, one of the main roles of the American public schools was to Americanize and assimilate its foreign students and children of immigrants, while deepening native children's connection to America and its culture.

The importance of "being American" can be traced back directly to the immediately post-Revolutionary era when the founding fathers of the new republic went to great lengths to distance themselves from their British ancestry, and reestablish their identities as Americans. Such examples of these efforts came in the form of the publication of *Webster's Speller*, written by Noah Webster, which respelled English words into American English versions, such as *musick* now spelled as *music* and *honour* now spelled as *honor*. A similar sentiment from an eighteenth-century newspaper claims that

> as the child of the foreigner plays with his school fellow, he learns to whistle "Yankee Doodle" and "Hail Columbia" and before he leaves the school-desk for the plough the anvil or the trowel, he is a sturdy little republican as can be found in the land.[1]

The formal establishment of public schools, especially during the time of Horace Mann, is likely the site of the deepest and most systematic infusion of Americanization in schools, and one that was to be inextricably linked to the Protestant ethic. It was Mann's main purpose to center the school itself on the Protestant ethic, which he believed to be both identical to and contributive of the American ethic. On a number of occasions Mann claims to be interested in depoliticizing schools by focusing its curriculum on teaching children to be "American."[2] He did so by centering the new curriculum on largely mytholo- gized and sterilized versions of the founding fathers related in a storytelling manner that was accessible and memorable to children.

However, it is imperative to remember that, to Mann, being American and being Protestant were mutually dependent. That is, the virtues of freedom, liberty, and individuality were not as much American as they were Protestant, but rather were American *because* they were Protestant. This, Mann believed, was the key to creating a society in which education can be the equalizing fac- tor and fulfill the goals of the American experiment. As he states, "Education, beyond all other devices, is the equalizer of the conditions of men, the great balance wheel of the social machinery."[3]

Mann's infusion of Protestantism, which invariably became interchange- able with American middle-classism, remained central to the growing and deepening culture of the common American public school. As attendance in schools increased, especially among poor black children, as well as for- eign children and children of immigrants, the social need to Americanize students took a deep hold. With two major wars fought by the middle of the twentieth century, both of which included large American investments of soldiers and money, the sense of nationalism became overwhelming. While the prior decades of educational theory were amenable to socialist-leaning philosophies such as those from George S. Counts and John Dewey, the mid- century zeitgeist no longer tolerated any such rhetoric or philosophy deemed "anti-American."[4]

The most imposing form of nationalism came under the auspices of Sena- tor Joseph McCarthy, and eventually became so engrained in the times that it gained the moniker "McCarthyism." One of the central institutions upon which suspicion was cast was the public school, seen not only as the place in which American children should learn to be "American," but the place in which all sentiments perceived as "anti-American" should be prohibited. By 1950, in this vein, 33 states had adopted legislation providing a means by which to terminate teachers seen as "disloyal" or "anti-American." Further, 26 states required teachers to take a "loyalty oath," a practice deemed consti- tutional by the Supreme Court in 1952.[5]

This hysteria was not to be limited just to Americans who were questioning the dominant cultural narrative, but also to black children, as well as foreign children and children of immigrants. Using the euphemism "culturally deprived," emerging social scientists and education scholars were charged to determine methodologies that could infuse middle-class standards within non-white cultures. Examples of this effort were the adoption of the widely popular McGuffey Readers, which presented similar mythologized and ster- ilized accounts of Columbus, the founding fathers, the Civil War and other events in American history a la Mann, as well as the practice of reciting the "Pledge of Allegiance" (including the addition "under God" under the Eisenhower administration) at the start of each school day.[6,7]

Essentially, the central role of the school in the 1950s became to reinforce American values into American children, as well as to assimilate those children who were "culturally deprived," "non-American," or "non-white" into viewing the middle-class, Protestant American ethic as the standard toward which to strive. In a tacit but powerful way, ideological hegemony centered on the middle-class ethic became the cornerstone of American curriculum. As Katz suggests, "The anxiety about cultural heterogeneity propelled systems of public education; from the very beginning public schools became agents of standardization."[8]

The increasing urbanization of the country added to the perceived necessity of Americanization. With neighborhoods becoming increasingly multicultural and the potential for the influence of foreign traditions and value systems threatening the fabric of America, still reeling from the economic Depression of the 1930s and struggling with its own racial relations, there was a strong cultural sense of the need for nationalism.

Contemporaneously affecting the conversation was the growing influence of social science. Though in many ways framed within a more liberal context, the main thrust of the social science narrative was that poverty was indicative not of a deep-seated and systematic institutional problem, but rather an indication of personal defect. Extending from this notion is the idea that if there were a group of people that were globally affected by poverty, these people should be thought of as generally responsible for their economic situation based on some level of cultural defect, especially in a capitalistic system that purportedly valued, and deeply believed in the equalizing mechanisms of a "free market."

The solution was, as it nearly ubiquitously is, a financial investment framed in the Elementary and Secondary Education Act (1965) (ESEA), which provided funds to allow schools to meet the "special educational needs" of culturally deprived children. That is, it is not that the cultural values of groups that were challenged to meet the middle-class ethic were evaluated and incorporated into the school system that was supposedly "for all," but rather that they would be given assistance in order to find ways to "improve" what they had been failing to do: bringing children "up to the standard" while simultaneously discarding their cultural defects that prevented their assimilation and social mobility.

Essentially, the neoliberal social movement in education was begun with ESEA, which maintained that the "white, middle-class" way of living was correct, and that black children would be able to learn to meet that standard, if only they had the resources to do so. In this a very clever and common neoliberal mechanism is employed: the general message of the reform revolves around amelioration of social ills and social justice, while the hegemony of the middle class is maintained. That is, it is not entirely "their fault" that they are not up to "our level," so *we*, as the privileged and dominant, are obliged to provide the help *they* need to get there.

The public school, then, became not only the central site of producing an educated class, but also the site of controlling how and with what information the educated class is indoctrinated. The democratic notions of Adams and Jefferson regarding schooling, though potentially overly romanticized in and of themselves, were essentially lost in translation. Rather than schools being the sites of social, political, and cultural agency, they became the centers of social, political, and cultural control.

Whether the dominant educational philosophy was to use schools to secure one's place of economic contribution or to exercise one's mind as a muscle through classic forms of study, the notion of equalization in its purer sense was no longer of value. Rather, school was to become the gatekeeper of who would and would not enter the mainstream society as a generally free agent, and whose narrative would be maintained as the "correct one."

The proverbial social gauntlet was essentially "thrown down," and it was based entirely on the attainment of the middle-class standards of living. It is this referential of the middle-class standard to which all elements of public schooling success is to be compared, and it is upon the most unlikely children to which it will be held most firmly. It is this reference to middle-class standards from which academic standards came.

Those very seemingly liberal pleas of Kennedy, Johnson, Clinton, and Obama and their counterpart conservative pleas from Nixon, Reagan, H. W. Bush and W. Bush both hold the same frame of reference: that it is the responsibility of those who do not meet the middle-class standard to do so or suffer justifiable marginalization, if not outright social exclusion. The narrative went: "Never mind your own cultural values, your own cultural perspectives, and the means by which you have been marginalized and excluded from the American story save for one or two gratuitous and ceremonious gestures—you must meet the standard."

With this the many cycles and circles of education reform began, all of which held these middle-class standards, be they measured by scores on achievement tests, high school graduation rates, college entrance, or Graduate Equivalency Degree (GED) attainment (which is also sold and controlled by a private corporation).

Seldom, if ever, was part of the question what each different culture believed their contribution to the narrative should be; what their perception of the middle-class ethic was; whether their culture valued the same elements as the culture to which they were being taught to assimilate; whether, even if they did believe it, the conditions in their schools and qualifications of their teachers would be able to get them there. This is the perpetual state of individuals who belong to a marginalized culture, and it is maintained, if not capitalized on, by the burgeoning American plutocracy.

If the central tenet in a belief system is maintained around the unequal standing of one culture toward another, and the equality of those unequal cultures can come only when the standard of the dominant culture is met, there can never truly be equality. In this sense, perhaps it is not equality that the school system should strive for. Indeed, equality indicates that everyone gets the "same" thing.

Perhaps, rather, it is accessibility to and inclusiveness in the narrative and the curriculum that the schools should strive for. That is, providing less emphasis on *giving* marginalized groups what they had not received before, so long as it stays under the control of the powerful, but more in terms of providing them the resources, community investment, and cultural support they need to ensure that their beliefs, value systems, and stories make their way into the lives of all American children, regardless of whether they are a part of their direct neighborhood or not.

Assimilation, then, must be seen as no less than abusive, a state of forced compliance by which one must choose to acquiesce or to be denied education. Essentially, this is what the current state of education is. Regardless of whatever the euphemism in which the message remains cloaked, the central message remains unchanged: assimilate or be systematically excluded by any means necessary.

When we insist that our students learn from particular books, focus on particular subjects, be assessed in particular ways that pay no mind to cultural narratives, speak in a particular manner using particular words, inflections, and accents that are preapproved and indicative of being American, we have essentially denied them their true right to cultural citizenship and have violated what it should mean to be American in the twenty-first century. The plutocracy has stolen our freedom.

NOTES

1. The Minnesota Chronicle and Register. Retrieved on September 28, 2015 from https://archive.org/stream/americansallimmi00unit/americansallimmi00unit_djvu.txt.

2. Diane Ravitch, *The Troubled Crusade: American Education 1945–1980.* (New York: Basic Books, 1985).

3. Horace Mann, cited in Sarah Mondale, *School: The Story of American Public Education* (New York: Beacon, 2000).

4. Ravitch, *The Troubled Crusade.*

5. Ravitch, *The Troubled Crusade.*

6. Mondale, *School.*

7. Kevin M .Cruse, *One Nation under God.* (New York: Basic Books, 2015).

8. Michael B. Katz, "The Origins of Public Education: A Reassessment." *History of Education Quarterly*, 16 no. 4, (1976), 381–407.

Chapter 3

Public Peril and Corporate Promise

Civil Rights, School Choice, and the Panacea of Privatization

In a capitalistic society there is ever a tension between the private sector and the public, as those who participate in the private sector are also just as much a part of the public as those who do not. While this tension is apparent in virtually all aspects of the public sphere, one of the more contentious grounds is that of public schooling. From a governmental standpoint, these tensions have become far less distinct given the reemergence of neoliberalism and its general acceptance of corporate influence in public domains (indeed, this reliance on corporate support may be neoliberalism's most distinguishing factor), as well as its alarmist perspective of the American public, for which private intervention is deemed the only real remedy. The cause of the public education crisis from this perspective is clear and present: low expectations and mediocrity of teachers complicated by unnecessary protections of tenure and nonmeritocratic pay by unions.

Ravitch rightfully suggests that the media plays an integral role in this distinction, with well-funded and publicized productions such as *Waiting for Superman*[1] and *The Lottery*[2] propagating this perspective. As she suggests:

> In Hollywood films and television documentaries, the battle lines are clearly drawn. Traditional public schools are bad; their supporters are apologists for the unions. Those who advocate for charter schools, virtual schooling, and "school choice" are reformers; their supporters insist that they are championing the rights of minorities. They say they are the leaders of the civil rights movement of our day. It is a compelling narrative. . . . There is only one problem. . . . It is wrong.[3]

Ravitch's criticism, though disputed fervently by those in support of school choice through privatization, clearly holds true when the more comprehensive story of the educational privatization movement is exposed. In Ravitch's understanding, the rhetoric of the public schooling crisis and both the subtle and blatant discrimination and underserving of minority children, though in some cases true, is not being proffered for altruistic means of social melioration and social justice. Rather, this populist rhetoric of civil rights, choice, and discrimination is used as a device to turn the public against its own schools and entrust its reform to those already in power and with the most means of political influence and financial strength: the corporate elites. As Ravitch goes on to say:

> [The corporate elite] want the public to believe that our public schools are a clear and present danger to our society. Unless there is radical change, they say our society will fall apart. Our economy will collapse. Our national security is in danger. The message is clear: public education threatens all that we hold dear.[4]

The most significant and useful rallying cry of this movement is the notorious "achievement gap." This pernicious divide between the performance of minority and white students has been capitulated and recapitulated in a myriad contexts, from educational legislation to reform rhetoric to pleas for increased funding. It is, undoubtedly, a true phenomenon, but one that has been bastardized and exploited by the privatization movement in education for reasons that serve no other purpose than the destruction of public schools and the ultimate replacement of them by independent, deregulated, decentralized schools, which continue to be supported by public funds while generating profit for the private sector.

By placing all of the blame on schools for perpetuating the achievement gap, the vilification effort by the privatization movement becomes far easier, and provides a very useful foundation for their alternative: charter schools and vouchers. As Timar and Maxwell-Jolly suggest:

> One reason [for the persistent achievement gap] is that although schools can be held accountable for some of the disadvantage these students experience, they have been given the entire responsibility for closing the achievement gap. Yet the gap is the symptom of larger social, economic, and political problems that go far beyond the reach of the school. . . . While schools are part of the solution, they alone cannot solve the problem of educational disparities.[5]

Essentially, the rhetoric surrounding the justification of privatization is based squarely on the notion of school choice; another populist claim proffered by the privatization movement, which suggests that there is an inherent inequality in school accessibility. That is, wealthy families have an ever-present option of school choice by not only possessing the means to utilize private schools, but for having virtually no restrictions on where they choose to reside, allowing them to include the quality of schools as a factor in their residential decision-making process, and accept or reject particular options based on such a factor. Because lower-income, largely minority families are disallowed such residential freedom, the school choice offered by charter schools and voucher systems can serve as an equalizing force addressing this social and economic disparity.[6]

Joseph Nathan, a vocal school choice advocate, legitimates this point of view:

> This nation already has a massive school choice program favoring wealthy families. Federal and, in most places, state tax policies permit deductions for real estate taxes and for home mortgage interest. This means tremendous tax advantages for wealthy families, which can and have moved out of inner cities and into suburbs. The price of admission to many "public" suburban schools is the ability to purchase a home with hundreds of thousands or even millions of dollars and to pay real estate taxes. Wealthy families already have a choice, and they use it![7]

The trend toward economically supporting school choice was being increasingly realized by the government through the end of the twentieth and the beginning of the twenty-first century, leading to the availability of two major options, one of which would vastly outperform the other: voucher systems and charter schools. Both would be the means of increasing the privatization of the entirely public system of schooling, while maintaining the public funding for the schools.

In the case of vouchers, a system designed by Nobel laureate and University of Chicago economist Milton Friedman, the government would grant each family a voucher, or certificate with a predetermined monetary value with which they could pay for tuition to the school of their choice, be it public or private, including parochial schools. While the main impetus for this system grew largely out of the dispute between Catholic schools and local and state governments involving what the Catholic schools' share of the public school funds should be, this system of almost unfettered school choice purportedly allowed each family to enjoy the benefit of public money without being forced into attending a particular school based solely on geographical residency and zoning laws.

While deemed sensible by a number of supporters, especially conservatives who were concerned with growing influence of both state governments and the federal government in matters of schooling, this system was also highly criticized by civil rights advocates on a number of accounts. First, vouchers do not equalize family positions in schooling. While each family would get a standard amount of money from the government, there were little regulations to stop families from supplementing their vouchers with their own money allowing, essentially, tuition assistance for attendance at elite schools that are inaccessible to poorer families even with scholarship and voucher opportunities. Second, a number of critics were suspicious of the system's ability to be used as a loophole for desegregation efforts by allowing white families to opt for attendance in schools that were unlikely to be integrated.

Though popular among a number of politicians, voucher legislation was almost never passed, providing little opportunity for the system to be utilized or vetted. Some years later, beginning in the late 1980s and not coming to full fruition until the early 1990s, the notion of charter schools came to replace that of vouchers as the system best suited to facilitate school choice for struggling families.

Originating as an idea from Ray Budde, a professor at the University of Massachusetts, Amherst, as well as Albert Shanker, the storied teacher union leader, charter schools were initially conceptualized as extensions of public schools in which students who were disengaged, unresponsive, or even dropped out of public schools would be given an opportunity to work with choice teachers under little regulatory control. In these schools, teachers were free to be creative, unorthodox, and collaborative, in order to determine alternative ways to reach students who did not benefit from more traditional forms of schooling.

They were, however, in the conceptualization of Budde and Shanker, intended to be entirely staffed by public school teachers and supported by public school funds—quite literally an extension of the public school system. They were not devised to be alternative, independent schools that were subcontracted to private entities and utilized for profiteering.[8] Neither were they intended to be competitive with the traditional public school.

However, as the privatization movement was reeling from the failure of vouchers, the concept of charter schools began to become increasingly appealing to private investors who were seeking new and lucrative ways to diversify their investment portfolios. The worsening strain of economic deterioration and the consistent elimination of school funding efforts at both the federal and state levels provided an environment that was ripe for the private sector to begin taking both financial and managerial interest in public schools that were desperate for increased funding. Thus began the conversion of what was intended to be an extension of public school to serve those who were struggling in traditional school settings into the financial investment opportunity of the twenty-first century for the rich, and the most significant threat to the public nature of schooling since its inception in the mid-1800s: the contemporary charter school.

To capitalize on this opportunity, the largely nebulous concept of school choice was deftly employed to frame the justification for and even necessity of the privatization of education movement, with the tautology being simple and clear:

a. students are required to attend their zoned public school should they not be attending a private school;
b. public schools are failing;
c. the failure of public schools combined with geographical zoning laws are causing students to be bound to underperforming schools based on their geographical location;
d. privatization efforts toward public school management can relieve this cyclical failure by increasing resources and, thus, competition among schools;
e. competition, combined with school choice, will allow students to bypass discriminatory zoning practices and attend productive and high-achieving public schools.

Again, while the message is steeped in social justice and civil rights rhetoric and does make good sense from such a theoretical perspective, three main challenges to the rhetoric have come to threaten the very notion of privatization. First, the privatization movement appears to rely almost entirely on standardized measures as the singular tool for measuring achievement. This reliance has been shown, from a number of perspectives, to be both an oversimplification of performance and school effectiveness as well as a vastly imperfect measurement.

Second, the data simply do not support the idea that school choice results in higher achievement (even if using the movement's own imperfect litmus of achievement, the standardized assessment). Third, school choice does not appear to address the issues of segregation and zoning problems highlighted by its advocates, a fact most notably demonstrated by equally as discriminatory school choice methodologies (such as lotteries based on zip code) and, in many instances, has been shown to actually exacerbate it.[9]

While it is unfair and inaccurate to accuse all supporters of charter schools as being pundits for the privatization effort of public schooling, as it is clear that many of the earlier advocates were not, it is fair to say that, despite the genuine intention of some proponents of the charter school idea, it has been usurped by the callous, mendacious, and mercenary private sector. Though their rhetoric continues to be couched in terms of civil rights, social justice, educational achievement, school reform, and school choice, further analysis will reveal that the charter school movement has become little more than a promising investment opportunity for wealthy venture capitalists (some of whom now deem themselves venture philanthropists[10,11]), motivated by profit and generous tax breaks.

NOTES

1. Davis Guggenheim (2010) http://www.imdb.com/title/tt1566648/.

2. Madeleine Sackler (2010) www.thelotteryfilm.com .

3. Diane Ravitch, *Reign of Error: The Hoax of the Privatization Movement and the Danger to America's Public Schools* (New York: Vintage, 2014), 4.

4. Ibid., 34.

5. Thomas B. and Julia Maxwell-Jolly, *Narrowing the Achievement Gap* (Cambridge, MA: Harvard Education Press, 2012), 230.

6. Jennifer Jellison Holme (2002). "Buying Homes, Buying Schools: School Choice and the Social Construction of School Quality," *Harvard Educational Review*, 72 no. 2 (2002), 177–205.

7. Joseph Nathan. "Heat and Light in the Charter School Movement," *Phi Delta Kappan*, 79 (1995), 499–505.

8. Ravitch, *Reign of Error.*

9. Justine S. Hastings, Thomas J. Kane, Douglas O. Staiger. (2006). "Preferences and Heterogeneous Treatment Effects in a Public School Choice Lottery." http://www.nber.org/papers/w12145.

10. Eileen Cunnifee (2014). "Wait—What Is Venture Philanthropy Again?" *Nonprofit Quarterly*. Retrieved from https://nonprofitquarterly.org/2014/03/12/wait-what-is-venture-philanthropy-again/.

11. Kevin Kumashiro (2012). "When Billionaires Become Educational Experts." *Academe*. Retrieved from http://www.aaup.org/article/when-billionaires-become-educational-experts#.VpQW62M0_x4.

Chapter 4

One Nation under Corporatization

The Government and the Neoliberal Education Market

Partisan conflicts are not uncommon in American government, especially in the current era. Ideological lines are clearly drawn regarding issues such as marriage equality, marijuana legalization, and health care. However, one area that has typically received bipartisan support with little disagreement across liberal and conservative lines is education reform. While there is, indeed, a boundary to this agreement, the main themes of public crisis and private panacea remain consistent.

Perhaps one of the reasons for the general long-standing agreement across party lines regarding education reform, in particular, is the refocusing of the neoliberal economic perspective and its contemporary congruity with the classically conservative sense of private wealth. That is, neoliberalism maintains the belief that the government's role in the economy is as a facilitator of marketplace conditions, laws, and institutions which enable its operation, as well as in producing individuals that become entrepreneurs.[1] Specifically, a neoliberal market emphasizes the privatization of the public sector to fund initiatives that can be deemed as socially responsible. Such efforts are in service of preserving the greatness, if not exceptionality, of America.

Conservatives would generally support privatization efforts and concur with the notion of American exceptionalism. Though less likely to support the dispensation of some of these profits for use toward investment in minority communities and schools, increasing its entanglement with federal funding, the potential personal financial payoff and influence in government policy appeared to be enough of a carrot to lay these concerns aside, especially since said investment has become entirely insignificant.

While the private involvement in the public sector bears less of a contentious role between political parties and genera ideologies, perhaps the most distinct source of contention between neoliberals and conservatives is the role

21

and extent that federal (and even state) power should play in these generally private enterprises. While neoliberal theory tends to support the notion of limited government intervention, neoliberal administrations, especially that of Obama, have clearly departed from this classical liberal sentiment as the control of the federal government continues to be enhanced in a number of public arenas, especially that of education.

However, as the federal government has, on the one hand, extended the reach of governmental control of previously less controlled areas of the economy, it has also provided unprecedented opportunities for private investors and corporations to profit personally from being involved in these efforts. In this sense, the current state of the public school system represents the perfect condition of a prime neoliberal market that can also be supported by more conservative thinkers: its purposes are steeped in social responsibility, while its financial destitution makes it ripe for privatization. This composition of this neoliberal market and its successful usurpation of the education market is best explained by Michael Apple:

a. dominant neoliberal economic and political elites intent on "modernizing" the economy and the institutions connected to it;
b. largely white working-class and middle-class groups who mistrust the state and are concerned with the security, the family, and traditional knowledge and values, and who form an increasingly active segment of what might be called *authoritarian populists*;
c. economic and cultural neoconservatives who want a return to high standards, discipline, and social Darwinist competition;
d. a fraction of the new middle class who may not agree with these other groups but whose own professional interests and advancement depend on the expanded use of accountability, efficiency and management procedures that are their own cultural capital.[2]

The infrastructure for what has lately been termed the "education-industrial complex" has been developing for roughly four decades, likely beginning with Reagan's effort to decrease public spending while increasing private investment in public sectors.[3] While standardized testing has been endorsed by the federal government for quite some time, most notably the establishment of the National Assessment of Educational Progress (NAEP) in 1969, the Reagan administration sought to use the burgeoning testing industry to empower corporate America while disenfranchising teacher unions, as well as the Department of Education as a whole. By shifting the focus to standardized testing as a measure for student progress, the Reagan administration granted unprecedented access to corporations seeking to become more involved in the flourishing education business, while allowing them to receive federal monies for doing so.[4]

This level of interchange between public schools and private corporations continued under the administration of George H. W. Bush, most notably in the establishment of the New American Schools Development Corporation, jump-started by then CEO of IBM Louis Gerstner and funded entirely by public monies authorized by Congress. This group, responsible for the drafting of America 2000, the first explicit large-scale call sanctioned by the federal government to regard schools as corporations, would also benefit excessively from the sale of curricula, texts, and testing materials, not to mention consultation and technology investments necessary to meet such standards.

The increased emphasis on standards combined with then "voluntary" efforts to measure the progress toward them resulted in virtually all states in the union being involved, to one degree or another, in such corporate entanglement. Such entanglements were maintained under the Clinton administration by way of Goals 2000, which was virtually a copy of its predecessor, America 2000.

Perhaps the major watershed moment for this sector of the market was at the 1996 National Education Summit in Palisades, New York, when a new resource center to assist in the benchmarking process of state academic standards was established by Achieve, Inc., an organization led by governors and corporate leaders from around the United States. The emergence of such benchmarking endeavors led to the creation of a number of new tests used across the country, including the Iowa Test of Basic Skills, the Metropolitan Achievement Test, as well as the Gates-MacGinitie Reading Test and the Basic Early Assessment of Reading, all of which are mainstays in educational evaluation protocols. Houghton Mifflin, who owns these tests, increased its profits by nearly 18 percent by the year 2000 as a result of this initiative.[5]

Additional partnerships between the government and corporate educational organizations can be found with Pearson Education, which has a long involvement with the scoring of the NAEP (as does the Educational Testing Service, which owns the NAEP and subcontracted its scoring to Pearson for several years). After its acquisition of National Computer Systems in 2000, Pearson officially became the largest scoring organization in the United States.[6] Also virtually monopolizing public school assessments in the advent of the Common Core State Standards (CCSS) as well as on several states' teacher certification examinations (the Teacher Performance Assessment, or edTPA), Pearson has acquired a virtual monopoly over the education reform market. And they intend to keep it this way. According to Todd Farley, longtime leader in the standardized testing industry and one-time Pearson consultant:

> The first thing I noticed on my first day at the Pearson scoring center in Phoenix was the intense emphasis on security. I don't mean on physical security. . . . I mean *corporate security* [italics in original]. . . . On the building's main entrance

was a sign prohibiting all cameras and recording equipment. . . . Additionally, the Pearson scorers had to sit through a lengthy human resources orientation that first day, and it included both the signing of confidentiality agreements promising to keep mum about the company's inner workings *and* a discussion on how to deal with intrusive media types who might be snooping around.[7]

These early initiatives became the very grounds upon which the initial systematic and efficient governmental assault on public schools, the No Child Left Behind Act (NCLB, 2001), took effect. This legislation purportedly centered on accountability for school performance, which not only mandates the use of standardized tests to assess student achievement, but also allows the unprecedented inclusion of charter schools as an option for parental school choice, if the school their child attends is deemed as failing for three consecutive years.

Unsurprisingly, these charter schools, which were now officially an option which would be funded by the public schools' budget, experienced a vast increase in revenue, as did educational testing and curriculum material companies such as McGraw-Hill, Houghton Mifflin, and Pearson. A number of the corporations that were most successful were soon identified as those with financial investment ties directly to the Bush family.[8] In fact, a very lengthy history of nepotism can be found between the Bush family and the McGraw-Hill corporation.[9] Interestingly, contemporaneously with the law reflecting charter schools as a viable option for school choice, the Department of Education established the Credit Enhancement for Charter School Facilities Program, which made competitive grants accessible to organizations or individuals seeking funds to invest in charter schools.[10]

It was surprisingly under the Obama administration, however, that the incestuous relationship between the educational branch of the public sector and corporate America was to be linked inextricably and at the most significant expense to the public. While during his initial campaign for president, Obama featured Linda Darling-Hammond, noted education scholar and professor at Stanford University, as his top education adviser and unmistakably considered her as a main contender for secretary of education, he ultimately chose Arne Duncan, a businessman backed by the Democrats for Educational Reform[11] lobby, with no classroom experience, but who was the former CEO of the Chicago Public school system, one of the most segregated and blighted city school systems in the country.

While less obvious to the public and the educational community at the time, the trend of Obama's administration toward education became glaring as it progressed. As CEO of the Chicago Public school system, Duncan, along with the then mayor Richard Daley, pushed an initiative known as Renaissance 2010, in 2004. This program, designed in collaboration with the Commercial Club of Chicago, a group comprised of local corporate, financial, philanthropic, and civic organizations, pledged to close under-performing public schools and replace them with "autonomous" schools by 2010. As promised, Renaissance 2010 implemented massive school closings, displacing children, largely from public housing projects, while their white, middle-class suburban counterparts were, in turn, lured to the city to partake in the new autonomous schools (some known euphemistically as "magnet schools").

To make room for more desirable students in these new "autonomous schools," the local children (primarily black) were bussed to other schools outside of their designated school zone. In total, there were 57 autonomous schools established: 42 of them were backed by corporate funds, three were initiated by teachers, nine were community centered, and three were sponsored by universities. Additionally, this initiative correlated positively with an increase in youth violence in the respective city areas in which children were displaced, likely because many of the now displaced students took no interest in attending new schools that were more difficult to travel to, and instead engaged in vagrancy, gang activity, and other deleterious draws of an inner city, all of which were more enticing and socially beneficial than school.[12]

The deep entanglements between the government and corporate America continued once Duncan was officially the secretary of education. Duncan appointed Joanne Weiss, a successful businesswoman with ties to a venture capital firm that heavily invested in charter schools, as his Chief of Staff. Weiss later became Duncan's main champion of his signature innovation, Race to the Top. About the initiative, Weiss noted on the Harvard Business Review Blog Network:

> The development of common standards and shared assessments radically alters the market for innovation in curriculum development, professional development, and formative assessments. Previously these markets operated on a state-by-state basis. . . . But the adoption of common standards and shared assessments means that education entrepreneurs will enjoy national markets where the best products can be taken to scale.[13]

In this statement Weiss made it unabashedly clear that the goal for Race to the Top was not, as it was marketed to the public, an innovation for education reform, but rather an innovation to stimulate business for entrepreneurs and corporations alike, using $4.5 billion of public funds to do so. Soon after, the conditions of qualification for Race to the Top funds were changed to include a mandate on the lifting of charter school limits within state legislatures, resulting in 42 states changing their existing charter laws in order to maintain qualification.

What followed was an influx of private entities and business elites, many of whom had close political and financial ties to major government figures, weighing in and contributing substantively to charter school policy and legislation in multiple states. Perhaps the most significant example of this was the American Legislative Exchange Council (ALEC), a group of primarily conservative state legislators and business leaders who promote agendas for large-scale privatization efforts and corporate interests in the public domain. ALEC formally proposed a policy document called the *Next Generation Charter Schools Act*, which delineated four fundamental aspects of charter schools:

1. Charter schools are considered public schools and are funded through public monies Charter schools should be exempt from most state laws and regulations as applied to traditional public schools.
2. Charter schools may be authorized by multiple agencies.
3. The governor should have power to override vetoes for chartering by local school boards.

This act brings to light the very hypocrisy of the charter school theory. First, though charter schools are to be considered public schools, and therefore funded by public monies, ALEC makes it clear that they may be governed, managed, and financially overseen by private boards not accountable to the local and state governments. Additionally, they may receive monetary and material donations by private interests. Second, charter schools, though claiming to be established to serve the community, seek to skirt the very protections mandated by such communities through governmental safeguards by insisting on being unaccountable to its laws and regulations. Additionally, charter schools remain exempt from public oversight by undermining districts' community elected boards of education by seeking authorization elsewhere.

Finally, while many organizations such as ALEC oppose governmental control in most areas including education, they support the governor's involvement when it can benefit their agenda. These foundations became increasingly important during the second decade of the new millennium, as much of ALEC's wording has been adopted nearly verbatim in some states such as North Carolina, and very closely mirrored in the charter law of others, such as New Jersey.

Ultimately, since the spirit of Race to the Top came largely out of Obama's America's Recovery and Reinvestment Act, an initiative to stimulate a waning domestic economy, the deal was sweetened even further, not for the states, but for private corporations who were interested in capitalizing on the new lucrative educational market. Namely, through a relatively obscure tax code called the New Markets Tax Credit (NMTC), investors in charter schools and other facets of the education market (among other community-based markets) could receive significant tax benefits. As touted by the Department of Treasury, NMTC is an effort by

> the private sector and the federal government to bring economic and community development to low income communities. From job creation to increased access to essential educational, health, and retail services, and from the rehabilitation of blighted communities to the development of renewable energy sources, NMTC projects have benefited neighborhoods throughout the country.[14]

According to Juan Gonzales, reporting for Democracy Now!, investors who take advantage of this program are able to double their investment in as few as seven years.[15]

Essentially, the new and financially alluring education-industrial complex has been boosted largely by what Naomi Klein refers to as "disaster capitalism," which is the orchestration of raids implemented on the public sphere by the private sector in the wake of catastrophic events transformed into new investment opportunities.[16] The catastrophe in this case was the nationwide failure of America's public schools and its dire threat on our economy, security, and fate as a nation. David Brain, head of the Entertainment Properties Trust, a multibillion dollar enterprise, describes charter schools as

> a very high-demand product. There's 400,000 kids on waiting lists for charter schools. . . . The industry's growing about 12–14% a year. So it's a high-growth, very stable, recession-resistant business. It's a public payer, the state is the payer on this . . . and if you do business with states with solid treasuries, then it's a very solid business.[17]

Lest one thinks that these perks are reserved for American investors only, a federal program known as EB-5 allows foreign entities who invest $500,000 or more in American charter school companies become eligible to purchase immigration visas for both themselves and their families.[18]

In the end, it is clear that though both the pro-privatization government and the private sector has couched its purported concerns about education in populist rhetoric, the interest in enhanced educational reform has served one purpose only: profiteering, and doing so at the public's expense. While the government has been entrusted to serve and to protect its constituents by acting on their behalf, the now pervasive and corruptive influx of both neoliberal and neoconservative corporatization has commoditized the nation's true greatest resource, its children, to its least contributive entity, the corporation.[19,20,21]

According to Americans for Tax Fairness, a watchdog group, the corporate share of the federal tax in America has dropped from 32 percent in 1952 to just 10 percent in 2013, with some of the largest companies paying no income taxes at all between 2008 and 2013. While many opponents of this characterization cite the top statutory rate, or the tax contribution required by law (which is 35%), data suggest that the effective tax rate, or the rates actually paid by corporations are drastically less to the US government, with some studies actually showing these companies paying higher rates to other countries.[22]

Todd Farley summarizes it best when he states:

> What does it mean to entrust decisions about this country's students, teachers, and schools to the massive standardized testing industry? In my opinion, it means trusting an industry that is unashamedly in the business of making money instead of listening to the many people who went into education for the more altruistic desire to do good.[23]

NOTES

1. Michelle Salazar Perez and Gaile S. Cannella, *Childhoods: A Handbook* (New York: Peter Lang, 2010).

2. Michael Apple (1996) cited by Lesley Bartlett, Maria Frederick, Thadeus Gulbrandsen, and Enrique Murillo. "The Marketization of Education: Public Schools for Private Ends," *Anthropology & Education Quarterly*, 33 no.1 (2002), 1–25.

3. Pepi Leistyna. "Corporate Testing: Standards, Profits, and the Demise of the Public Sphere." *Teacher Education Quarterly*, Spring 2007: 59–84.

4. Ibid.

5. Ibid.

6. Ibid.

7. Todd Farley, *Making the Grades: My Misadventures in the Standardized Testing Industry*. (San Francisco: Berrett-Keohler Publishers, 2009), 163.

8. Leystina. "Corporate Testing."

9. Stephen Metcalf (2002), "Reading between the Lines." *The Nation*. From http://www.thenation.com/article/reading-between-lines.

10. Richard Mora and Mary Christianakis, "Charter Schools, Market Capitalism, and Obama's Neo-liberal Agenda." *Journal of Inquiry & Action in Education*, 4 no. 1, (2011), 93–111.

11. DFER was an organization comprised of Wall Street investors, who have clear political ties to the Democratic Party and contribute generously to campaigns.

12. Mora and Christianakis, "Charter Schools."

13. Joanne Weiss, cited by Diane Ravitch, *Reign of Error*, p. 14

14. Kristin Rawls, "Who Is Profiting from Charters? The Big Bucks behind Charter School Secrecy, Financial Scandal, and Corruption." http://www.alternet.org/education/who-profiting-charters-big-bucks-behind-charter-school-secrecy-financial-scandal-and.

15. Ibid.

16. Naomi Klein, *The Shock Doctrine*, 2007, New York: Picador.

17. Valerie Strauss, "The Big Business of Charter Schools," *The Washington Post*, August 17, 2012 https://www.washingtonpost.com/blogs/answer-sheet/post/the-big-business-of-charter-schools/2012/08/16/bdadfeca-e7ff-11e1-8487-64e4b2a79ba8_blog.html.

18. Allison Wiggin, "Charter School Gravy Train Runs Express to Fat City." *Forbes*, http://www.forbes.com/sites/greatspeculations/2013/09/10/charter-school-gravy-train-runs-express-to-fat-city/.

19. Susan Ohanian. (2002). *What Happened to Recess and Why Are Our Children Struggling in Kindergarten?* McGraw-Hill Education.

20. Diane Ravitch. (2014). "Public Education: Who Are the Corporate Reformers." Retrieved from http://billmoyers.com/2014/03/28/public-education-who-are-the-corporate-reformers/.

21. "The Trouble with the Common Core" (2013). Retrieved from http://www.rethinkingschools.org/archive/27_04/edit274.shtml.

22. http://www.americansfortaxfairness.org/tax-fairness-briefing-booklet/fact-sheet-corporate-tax-rates/.

23. Farley, p. 242.

Chapter 5

Foundation for Fabrication

The Boisterous Rise and Tacit Failure of the Charter School

The rise of the charter school in the contemporary public education landscape is one that requires great care in its handling. Convoluted by multiple definitions, frameworks, and original intent for such alternative means of schooling, there is but one aspect of the charter school movement that remains clear: the current dominant version of the corporate-backed charter school stands in sharp contrast to what was initially envisioned by the great supporters of the public school.

While the basis for charter schools, even in the midst of growing privatization efforts, were sound, ethical, socially just and attempted to address some of the very real and trenchant problems facing traditional public schooling, the very purpose of these once sacred places of intervention has been bastardized to the point of corporate exploitation, and the most vulnerable children in America are paying the largest price.

As aforementioned, the concept of the charter school was initially proposed by Albert Shanker, the long-standing head of the United Federation of Teachers, and Ray Budde, a professor at the University of Massachusetts, Amherst, in the late 1980s. Charter schools were originally conceptualized as an alternative to traditional public schools, within which public school teachers would be given the creative and instructional freedom and curricular latitude to devise and implement unorthodox methods in order to reach disengaged, unresponsive, or even "dropped out" students.

These schools were not intended to serve as permanent, publicly funded private schools designed to be a fixture in the educational marketplace, but rather as ad hoc and ephemeral alternatives that were entirely individualized in order to "rehabilitate" and reengage struggling students, with the ultimate intention of reintroducing them to the traditional public school environment.[1] A popular and practical idea from its inception, Minnesota became the first state to pass a charter school law authorizing the establishment of certain schools that were not bound to the bureaucracy and legislation of traditional public schools, but were funded by public monies.[2]

Over time, a number of definitions and conceptualizations of charter schools emerged. According to Bruno Manno, a charter school is

> an independent public school of choice, given a charter or a contract for a specified period of time . . . to educate children according to the school's own design, with a minimum of bureaucratic oversight. It may be a new school, started from scratch, or an existing one that secedes from its school district. It is held accountable to the terms of its charter and continues to exist only if it fulfills those terms. As a public school of choice, it is attended by students whose families select it and staffed by educators who choose to teach in it.[3]

According to Joe Nathan, a noted charter school advocate, the charter school movement

> brings together four main ideas: (a) choice among public schools for families and their children; (b) entrepreneurial opportunities for educators and parents to create the kinds of schools they believe make the most sense; (c) explicit responsibility for improved achievement, as measured by standardized tests and other measures; and (d) carefully designed competition in public education.[4]

Proponents of the initial charter school movement drew heavily on the idea that the most significant impediment to educational reform was the entrenchment of traditional public schools in bureaucracy and politics. As such, an alternative system was needed in order to better serve economically challenged students, most of whom were minorities, who were seen as the most significant victims of the beleaguered traditional public school system.[5] According to Chester Finn:

> The principal impediments to successful reform are elements of the system itself, structural and political problems that block us from making the kinds of changes we most need and from installing on a large scale the bold reforms with the greatest likelihood of yielding markedly better results.[6]

However, it was not long before the potentially pure efforts of the charter school concept were usurped by the financial interests of corporate America. In 1993, a for-profit firm called Educational Alternatives was contracted by the city of Baltimore, Maryland, to take over nine failing public schools. While maintaining the philosophical orientation of charter schools, the agreement between the city and the firm permitted the company to actually profit from the investment of public monies.

In return for the contract, the company updated the physical plant of these schools and invested in new computers for student use, but also replaced qualified, certified, union-member teachers with less-qualified, nonunion teachers who were paid at a lower wage, adding a significant contribution to firm's profit margin for the project.

An additional example of corporate benefit from public monies is found with the Noah Webster Academy (NWA) in Detroit, Michigan. Resulting from an agreement involving the cooperation of a small, impoverished public school district which received $40,000 in the deal, control over their publicly funded budget was given to NWA, which used the public monies to create a network of nearly 700 mostly white homeschooled children and implemented a Christian-based curriculum.[7]

However, despite these early signs of corporatization and privatization as a result of the largely deregulated use of public monies, the promise of charter schools, even those established by corporate-backed sponsorships, remained intact, and strongly so. That deregulation, curricular freedom, exemption from state laws, and the continuance of public financial support of the charter school was to be the answer to the ills of the traditional public school system rang true to many, in both the public and private realms.

If this proposal was, indeed, true, is it not worth the sacrifice of even large amounts of public funds lining the pockets of some private entities in order to invest in a stronger future for American children? Many would likely say it is, and this belief was a major contributor in maintaining and growing the charter approach.

There was, however, one major problem with the premise: it was not working by any available measure. Despite the lofty promises of powerful brokers in the new educational reform movement, charter schools not only failed to remedy the public school situation, but significantly contributed to a large share of the social devolution now present in its wake, including resegregation, continuation of "low achievement," usurpation of public funds for immense private profit, and the propagation of even less supported public schools as a result of monies siphoned off to the charter system.

The significance of educational inequality based on racial grounds was a common cry of the early charter schools movement. The charge, as it was commonly brought, alleged that traditional public schooling was inherently unequal in the schools attended by minorities while predominantly white public schools were advantaged. Indeed, this was (and remains) quite true. However, what was conspicuously absent from the argument was a remediation to the very issue of segregation itself. The proponents of charter schools did not include a plan for better integration in their approach.

Indeed, multiple studies validate that the charter school movement has not only maintained segregation among black and Latino students, but has likely exacerbated it. In 2003, roughly 70 percent of all black charter school students attended "intensely segregated minority schools" as compared with 34 percent of black traditional public school students. White students in charter schools are more likely to attend schools with more non-white students than their counterparts in traditional public schools, though there are a number of "pockets" of white segregation in charter schools as well. The statistics were less clear for Hispanic and Latino students.[8]

Lest it is argued that over the next decade these statistics were likely to have changed, studies continue to indicate not only exacerbated segregation, but more exclusive selection processes of charter schools, adversely affecting English Language Learners and low-income students, as well as students with disabilities disproportionately. Based on data collected between 2007 and 2008, charter schools continue to isolate students based on race and class, demonstrating that charter schools in virtually every state are, indeed, *more* segregated than their traditional public school counterparts as evidenced by a number of research efforts.[9-12]

Notwithstanding the effects on resegregation, however, is it still fair to say that charter schools do, indeed, teach students more effectively, therefore resulting in higher achievement? The answer to this question remains resoundingly consistent as well: no. One of the earlier and most thorough examinations of this question came from a study sponsored by the Economic Policy Institute (EPI), published in 2005,[13] which addressed many of the claims of instructional and achievement superiority of charter schools made by proponents of the charter school movement.

This study was prompted largely in response to the claim made by members of the American Federation of Teachers, an organization in distinct opposition to charter schools, that data from the National Assessment of Educational Progress (NAEP) showed that: (1) students in public schools outperform those in charter schools; and (2) average achievement of black students is no better in charter schools than in traditional public schools.

In order to address the issue in a more systematic and scientifically based way, the authors of the EPI conducted an independent study to address the major points proffered by members of the charter schools movement, most specifically: (1) charter school students outperform students in traditional public schools; (2) charter schools are more accountable than traditional public schools; and (3) competition from charter schools will improve outcomes in traditional public schools.

Regarding the first claim of outperformance by charter school students, findings based on 19 studies conducted in 11 states and the District of Columbia suggested that not only were charter schools no better than traditional public schools in terms of achievement, but that traditional public school students actually outperformed those in charter schools to a significant degree.

In terms of the second claim, no evidence was found that accountability for student outcomes was stronger in charter schools. Lastly, there was no evidence to indicate that competition from charter schools motivates individual public school teachers or traditional public school systems as a whole to become more highly achieving, disconfirming the applicability of the corporate idea of competition to the functionality of public schools. While some studies suggest longitudinal success of charter schools,[14,15] there are a number of more current studies that continue to support these same conclusions.[16,17,18]

One particularly interesting study involves examining both the fiscal feasibility as compared to the instructional and achievement-based effectiveness of charter schools. As one of the main arguments in the charter school rhetoric, deregulation and less accountability for fiscal expenditures can result in a less bureaucratic system, allowing for quicker and more efficient delivery of instruction to students.

Therefore, charter schools are likely to create less of a strain on both public funds as well as bureaucratic processes. However, findings suggested that, though charter schools can, indeed, produce educational outcomes at a lower cost than traditional public schools, they are not systematically more efficient than traditional public schools. That is, cost-wise, charter schools pose an advantage, but achievement-wise, they do not. This, then begs the question: Is cost-saving without results more desirable than higher cost with better results? The answer to this question can accurately gauge where one's priority for reform truly is.

These failures of the privatization effort can, indeed, be demonstrated throughout history, most notably through the examples of the Texarkana project of the 1970s and the Edison Schools of the 2000s. In both of these instances, privatization efforts, disguised under two different initiatives, proffered the all-too-familiar notion that private wealth and corporate-style management can rectify the ills of public destitution, disorganization, and bureaucracy. However, in both the Texarkana and the Edison School cases (as is also demonstrated in a number of other examples not specifically mentioned) these ideas remained just that: lofty musings by the corporate elite, whose truth was never to come to be.

The first wide-scale privatization efforts in public schooling were applied in the Nixon era of the 1970s, when—like there is now—there was a surge in faith in the private sector, believing it to be capable of curing the ills of the public sector, especially public education. While the notion of "charter schools" in any sense was not yet conceived, the same foundational beliefs that underlie their justification were. The application of the principles appeared at the time under the concept and practice of "performance contracting."

Primarily the result of the appointment of Leon Lessinger, Nixon's associate commissioner of education and former member of the Aerospace

Foundation, schools were urged to utilize the services of private companies who were "pioneering" innovations in education. Texarkana, a small town that lies on the border between Texas and Arkansas, became one of the most well-known examples of this educational experiment, although it was only one of many.[19]

With financial assistance from a grant that was funded by the public monies available through the Elementary and Secondary Education Act (ESEA) the Texarkana school district contracted the services of Dorsett Educational Systems Inc., a small company based in Norman, Oklahoma, that manufactured audiovisual equipment. The contract between the private firm and the public district specified that roughly 350 remedial white and black students were to receive innovative instruction through a methodology developed by Dorsett. If the students receiving the Dorsett method of instruction showed significant gains in math and reading achievement, marked by reaching or exceeding grade level after 80 hours of instruction, Dorsett would earn its base payment, with additional payments to be made if students reached the goal in less than 80 hours. Further, Texarkana agreed to purchase equipment from Dorsett for use throughout their district.[20]

To fulfill the terms of the contract, Dorsett constructed well-equipped, air-conditioned trailers adjacent to the main school building in which the targeted students would spend two hours a day receiving instruction using machines called Rapid Learning Centers (RLCs). These machines employed instruction by using stimulus-response models in which students answered questions by pushing the corresponding buttons. Because the mechanism was built to respond to whether the student answered questions correctly (advancing only when they did), RLC was billed as "individualized instruction."[21]

Interestingly, a number of terms proffered by the ESEA grant as well as the contract with Texarkana changed during the implementation period, most notably that, since payment was contingent on gains in math and reading little, if any, instruction was focused on science and social studies, despite the initial agreement to do so. When it came time to assess the effectiveness of the RLC method, initial evaluations appeared to be favorable, indicating that the RLC students did, in fact, outscore those in the traditional model. However, it was soon revealed that the students in the RLC model were exposed to the test questions prior to evaluation, and the results were therefore disqualified.

Despite the failure of this first initiative, Texarkana entered into a more expensive agreement in its second year, this time with a different company called Educational Development Laboratories, Inc., which was a division of McGraw-Hill, a private publishing company with deep political ties. Interestingly, the new contract, though only in part tied to student performance gains, secured a higher base rate for McGraw-Hill that was not contingent on student performance at all, and received half of the monies upfront. [22]

By 1972, there were more than 150 performance contracts in effect between public school districts and private companies throughout the United States. As a response to this trend, the Office of Economic Opportunity (OEO) implemented a one-year study investigating whether there was, indeed, validity to the effectiveness of using private firms to reach educationally disadvantaged children.

After choosing six private companies at random, 18 districts were provided private investment, with the reward money paid to the respective private companies, contingent on gains in student performance. These gains would be compared to students in traditional public schools. At the culmination of the study, the results were clear, with data unequivocally indicating that there was no significant differences in the gains between the students in the performance contracted group and those in traditional public schools. Furthermore, performance fell far short of the levels promised by the companies or even the level needed to be achieved to remediate their deficiencies.

A more current example can be found with the Edison Schools, an educational management organization (EMO) founded by Chris Whittle, founder of Whittle Communications, Channel One News service, and *Esquire* magazine. Bearing few differences from previous privatization philosophies, Whittle believed that by applying business style management practices, privately run public schools (i.e., schools that are funded by public money but managed privately and with less regulation) could address educational inequities and increase academic outcomes, while also turning a profit (an aspect he was candid about) at the same cost of public schooling which, he claimed, did neither.

Through investment efforts provided entirely by private capital, Whittle composed a team of business leaders, technology experts, and, supposedly, education experts charged to design what would become known as the Edison model. The initial vision of the model was one that would be facilitated through a national network of private schools. Though the grander vision of a national network never materialized, an alternative plan of contracting with individual public school districts did,[23] in a basic design that did not differ much from the Texarkana and other "performance contracting" arrangements. The agreements resulted in the opening of its first four schools in 1995 in Boston, Massachusetts; Wichita, Kansas; Mt. Clemens, Michigan; and Sherman, Texas; followed by 58 new schools by 1999.

In November of 1999, Edison transitioned from a private to a publicly traded company, more than doubling its value per share of $18.00 in 1999 to $38.00 in 2001. This increase in revenue led to larger contracts across municipalities as well as higher rates of investment. In 2002, however, a complaint made to the Securities and Exchange Commission (SEC), though later settled, spurred a series of lawsuits bolstering public suspicion of Edison and other large-scale EMOs.[24] The Edison project became a marker of the ultimate impossibility of applying a corporate-style model, focused on reducing costs, increasing profit, and turning out performance to a public school system.

In order to sustain its growth and profitability through increased private and public investment, the Edison Schools became entirely focused on increasing student performance on standardized tests above all else. With all of the displaced pressure focused on assessment results rather than learning processes, the proposed culture of "achievement" and "efficiency" was replaced by an obsession with outcome, leading many teachers and students to cheat on the tests in order to ensure Edison's profitability.[25] Indeed, the promise of Edison turned out to be as unrealized as the promise of virtually all other privatization efforts that came before it, and would come since. While some studies did indicate better performance among Edison school students, the vast majority of studies did not, leaving the Edison project to be deemed ineffective at the large expense of the public, but largely profitable to its investors.[26]

The privatization and profiteering that has become endemic to charter school operations has detracted, if not entirely denigrated, the potential good that can come out of these likely initially well-intentioned ideas. If the focus of the charter schools movement was, truly, to serve a socially ameliorative purpose, there would likely be investment in the whole of the impoverished community, rather than just another means of drawing children out of it.

Indeed, the charter schools movement, as a whole, commits the same error that radical critics of public schooling and opportunist reformers have before: it centered both the blame and the solution for all social problems involving race and poverty on the schools alone. By doing so, its solution became an essential part of the overall failure by its deepening of segregation, heightening of teacher blame for all school ills, and its inability to return on its promise of higher achievement despite all of the so-called reforms and investments initiated.

Perhaps the ultimate lesson to extrapolate from what exists of the systematic analysis of charter school and traditional public school comparisons is that the philosophies and workings of neither should be disregarded. Indeed, the philosophical contributions of the charter school model, absent the influence of marketization and corporatization, provides a rational and sensible critique of traditional public schools. This amelioration should not be confused with gentrification of black and Hispanic communities, which serve to only displace poor Blacks and Hispanics and redistribute the property to the wealthy, as many other corporate "reinvestments" have done.

Rather, true socially ameliorative efforts could be achieved only by partnering with the community, including its leaders as main voices in the directions of the reinvestment, and making stronger public schools a major part, though not the only focus, of the reinvestment. As such, a refocusing on investing in public schools while applying the truly important lessons culled from the charter schools project is the most likely way to move forward while eliminating the mercenary intentions of the private sector.

NOTES

1. Ravtich, *Reign of Error.*

2. http://www.leg.state.mn.us/lrl/issues/issues?issue=charter.

3. Bruno Manno, as cited by Good and Braden, *The Great School Debate* (New York: Routledge, 1999), p. 119.

4. Joe Nathan. *Charter Schools: Creating Hope and Opportunity for American Education.* (San Fransisco, CA: Jossey-Bass, 1996).

5. John E. Chubb and Terry M. Moe. *Politics, Markets, and America's Schools.* (Washington, D.C.: Brookings Institution Press, 1990).

6. J. Chester Finn. "The Politics of Change." In D. Ravitch and J. Vitteri (Eds.) *New Schools for a New Century: The Redesign of Urban Education* (pp. 226–250). New Haven: Yale University Press.

7. Ravitch, *Reign of Error.*

8. Erica Frankenberg and Chungmei Lee. (2003). Charter Schools and Race: A Lost Opportunity for Integrated Education. Harvard Civil Rights Project, Cambridge, MA.

9. Erica Frankenberg, G. Siegel-Hawley, and J. Wang. "Choice Without Equity: Charter School Segregation." *Educational Policy Analysis Archives*, 19 no. 1, (2011). From http://epaa.asu.edu/ojs/article/view/779.

10. Gary Miron, Jessica Urschel, William J. Mathis, & Elana Tornquist (2010). Schools without Diversity: Educational Management Organizations, Charter Schools, and Demographic Stratification of the American School System. Education and the Public Interest Center & Education Policy Research Unit. From http://epicpolicy.org/publication/schools-without-diversity.

11. Robert Bifulco, Helen F. Ladd, and Stephen L. Ross. "Public School Choice and Integration Evidence from Durham, North Carolina. Social Science Research," 38 no. 1, (2009), 71–85.

12. Gary Orfield and Erica Frankenberg. *Educational Delusions?: Why Choice Can Deepen Inequality and How to Make Schools Fair.* (Los Angeles: University of California Press, 2013).

13. Martin Carnoy, Rebecca Jacobsen, Lawrence Mishel, and Richard Rothsetin. (2005). The Charter School Dust-Up. Washington, D.C.: Economic Policy Institute.

14. Jeffrey Henig. *What Do We Know about the Outcomes of KIPP Schools?* (East Lansing, MI: Great Lakes Center for Education, 2008).

15. Timothy R. Sass. "Charter Schools and Student Achievement in Florida." *Education Finance and Policy*, 1 no. 1, (2006), 91–122.

16. Robert Bifulco and Helen F. Ladd (2007). "School-choice, Racial Segregation, and Test-Score Gaps: Evidence from North Carolina's Charter School Program." *Journal of Policy Analysis and Management*, 26 no. 1, (2007), 31–56.

17. Helen F. Ladd. "Education and Poverty: Confronting the Evidence." *Journal of Policy Analysis and Management*, 31 no. 2, (2012), 203–227.

18. Christopher A. Lubienski and Sarah Theule Lubienski. *The Public School Advantage: Why Public Schools Outperform Private Schools* (Chicago: University of Chicago Press, 2013).

19. Carol Ascher. "Performance Contracting: A Forgotten Experiment in School Privatization." *Phi Delta Kappan*, 77 no. 9, (May, 1996) 615.

20. Ibid.

21. Ibid.

22. Ibid.

23. Julie A. Marsh, Ron W. Zimmer, Deanna Hill, and Brian P. Gill. "A Brief History of Edison Schools and a Review of Existing Literature." From *Inspiration, Perspiration, and Time. Brian P. Gill et al.* (Eds.). http://www.rand.org/content/dam/rand/pubs/monographs/2005/RAND_MG351.pdf .

24. Ibid.

25. Kenneth J. Saltman. (2009). "Putting the Public Back in Public Schooling: Public Schools beyond the Corporate Model." *DePaul Journal for Social Justice*, 3 no.1. (2009).

26. Marsh et al., "Brief History of Edison."

Chapter 6

Local Kids, Local Control

*Crafting the Decentralization of Schooling
across the World*

The significance of the role that globalization has come to play in relationships both within and between culturally diverse countries in the twenty-first century cannot be overstated. What remains unclear, however, is the most productive, constructive, and mutually respectful ways in which to address these globalization trends and efforts in a way that facilitates cooperation and collaboration rather than competition and supremacy. Schools and education, undoubtedly, appear to be at the center of virtually all countries' globalization efforts in what has become an unprecedented public attention being paid to many aspects of the public schooling process. One main area of debate remains the importance of centralization or decentralization of the public school system for increased efficiency (the definition of which varies between countries and cultures significantly).

It is argued that one of the clearest trends in emerging education reform policies internationally is decentralization, a trend that is not dissociated from the increasing belief that neoliberal organization is most amenable to increasing economic prosperity.[1] Though the tenets of neoliberal governance and market theory appear to favor decentralization, democracy, and accountability in its rhetoric, such as empowering local communities and local adoption of standards, the result of these efforts often take on largely centralized machinations.

Few countries, if any, have a more contradictory implementation of "decentralization" in schooling efforts than that of the United States. Despite a strong rhetoric of "local control" and "technical" separation between federal and state decision making in policy and legislation verbiage, current regulatory practices have increased the federal government's power and control over school financing, curricular choices, and accountability processes in an unprecedented manner.

Evidence of these contradictory practices between policy rhetoric and financial availability is no more obvious than in the Obama administration's rollout of the Race to the Top competitive grants. Though the frame for the grant was couched in local and independent "entrepreneurial" adaptations to its general tenets, the growing complexity of technicalities, such as that of the tacit requirement of adopting the Common Core State Standards (CCSS), lifting limits on the establishment of charter schools, and tying test scores to teacher evaluations cleverly yet effectively cinched the maintenance of federal government centralization in a camouflaged package of decentralization. It can now be argued that despite the amplification of the nearly ubiquitous decentralization rhetoric, education policies in the United States are more centralized than at any other time in its history.

Mexico's developing and rapidly changing educational policies share a common confusing and seemingly hypocritical history steeped in the same contradictions of a neoliberal market theory of schooling, much of which surrounds the unclear manner in which decentralization plays a role. While, for most of Mexico's history, there was staunch opposition to decentralization of schools, primarily due to the long history of Mexico as a corporatist state with strong nationalistic tendencies, the signing of the National Agreement for the Modernization of Basic Education in 1992 and the General Law of Education in 1993 distinctly changed the country's course.

Similar to efforts of education reform in America, the rhetoric of this law was purportedly to raise the quality of education and equity of access for all Mexican children.[2] Under this system, the state maintains most managerial duties over education including labor relations, curricular control, compensatory efforts, and other day-to-day concerns, so long as they adhere to the general standards of the SEP (Mexico's federal department of education). This shift in policy was highly politicized and ideological, with its main proponents praising decentralization efforts as being deeply rooted in democratic tradition and more aligned with the true spirit of Mexico's constitution (a familiar rhetoric to that of the American privatization effort).[3]

At first the decentralization efforts of Mexican public education appeared to be well-managed and preferable to teachers, despite the highly unionized and often corrupt previous system which was based largely on nepotism and political power playing. However, in the second decade of the twenty-first century, similar unrest to that of teachers in the United States began to be exhibited. As the neoliberal market theory took stronger hold in Mexico, in many ways as a result of the growing focus on economic prosperity, global competitiveness, and increased influence of American style governance and economic thought, the focus of Mexican education reform soon turned to "student performance and achievement" as measured by standardized tests, and a mode of reform that virtually mirrored the current American system.

This neoliberal market-based effort was entrenched even further with the granting of autonomy to the National Institute of Educational Assessment (INEE), which unilaterally created a new law that reassigned and redistributed administrative and teaching positions based on examination results as well as other largely meritocratic criteria.[4] Also, similarly to the education reform agenda in the United States, teachers played virtually no role in the crafting or adopting of new standards, assessment measures, or other aspects of the reform, creating an entirely top-down, corporate-style effort and resulting in, among other consequences, the striking of teachers and the closing of schools for several weeks in 2006 and again in 2015.[5]

Other countries, such as Poland, India, and Finland, have demonstrated more successful decentralization efforts, legitimately returning curricular power and decision latitude to the local community, as well as directly to teachers. For many of these countries, these large-scale educational reform efforts were part and parcel of greater social change projects, which is an important factor that will be handled more directly in a later chapter. However, common to the education reform efforts in these countries was not merely the rhetoric of decentralization guided by neoliberal market theory, but rather a genuine effort to redistribute policy and curricular decision-making latitude to the local arenas.

In the 1990s, after communism had fallen and the people of Poland were rebuilding their country in service of a more democratic structure, a sense of more powerful local control began to be favored as a direct response to the unilaterally centralized governmental system that was previously in place. Part of this effort was the initial establishment of *gminas*, or independently governed communities, which would systematically replace the centralized government, returning the rule directly to the people themselves. Endemic in this redistribution was the not-yet-created but future establishment of the *powiat*, or county-level, governmental system.

One of the most contested issues among the organization of these new communities was the responsibility over schools, which was, under communist rule, entirely controlled by the central government. Also complicating this notion was the maintenance of a national education department, known as the Ministry of National Education (MEN).[6]

At the beginning of the process, the proponents of localized government insisted that the *gminas* be responsible for preschool and primary education (secondary education was not yet compulsory in Poland) mainly in order to remove control of the schools from the grip of state bureaucrats. Eventually schools would likely come under the auspices of the *powiat* once they were established. However, the backlash almost immediately came from the strongly anticommunist though cautious members of the MEN who, despite supporting the idea of local control, were skeptical of the newly formed independent communities' ability to efficiently incorporate and manage a system of schooling at such an early phase of its existence.

Furthermore, the guiding philosophy of the MEN was to use schools as the main conduit for rebuilding a new sense of a unified national identity for the young culture. This act would be difficult, if at all possible, through independently governed local schools which ran the risk of creating a dis-unified plurality of potentially incompatible national identities. This sentiment of skepticism was also echoed by the Union of Polish Teachers.[7]

In the end, a convoluted set of compromises resulted in the immediate ownership of preschools by the *gminas*, while the ownership and control over primary schools would be initially maintained by the MEN and gradually transferred to the *gminas* systematically over a number of years. As part of this agreement, *gminas* were free to hire teachers and purchase supplementary educational materials such as language and computer programs, but were expressly prohibited from making their own pedagogical or directorial decisions, positions that were appointed and regulated by the MEN.

Though these unclear policies and power struggles between the new local governments and the remnant bureaucracy did, indeed, cause a number of problems including school closures, contentious labor relations, and unrest as to who paid for what services, virtually all schooling decisions were transferred, by 1999, to the now functional *powiats*, or county-level governments. Along with the transfer of the responsibility of schooling to the *powiats* came a redefinition of educational services, which would soon encompass special education schools, youth houses, diagnostic centers, and other comprehensive social service providers. Despite the tumultuous struggle to redefine and rebuild Poland's school system, it is now widely regarded as one of the most successful contemporary educational systems in the world.[8]

India's educational decentralization efforts also grew largely out of a more widely focused social agenda. In 1992, significant amendments were made to the Indian constitution in order to strengthen the latitude of the Local Self-Government Institutions, or local government agencies, one area of which was in education. This was a significant change from the previous legislation of 1972, which enacted a policy of shared responsibility of education between the state and federal governments. The main result was the launching of the District Primary Education Programme (DPEP), which sought to increase the efficiency and planning capabilities within Indian schools.[9]

Essentially, the DPEP grew out of improvements to previous efforts to decentralize and improve the Indian primary education system since its independence in 1947. Its efforts toward decentralization are based on three main initiatives.

First is the effort toward "creating facilitating conditions." These efforts include providing general guidelines for reframing but requiring uniform interpretation and implementation, ensuring financial support for each district level program, and providing total latitude to the individual districts for forming its own plan, including support for professional development and training at the district's discretion.

The second is "initiating the planning process." Generally regarded as being founded on professional and technical elements as well as participatory elements, this part of the initiative requires districts to devise clear and implementable plans with input from local stakeholders and experts such as teachers, academics, parents, and any other member of the general public, all of whom are regarded as potential stakeholders in education.

Third is "developing planning competencies." These competencies can be generalized in five broad areas including planning, research, improvement in pedagogical skills, program management, and monitoring, all of which are designed and implemented based on local input and planning.[10]

While large-scale reform effort of any kind is not without its challenges and struggles in implementation and results, the general perception of the effectiveness of the DPEP in India is largely positive. The decentralization philosophy created the means of participatory agency in educational decision making and stakeholding where it did not exist before. The efforts of decentralization effectively empowered local Indian communities to invest heavily in their schools and participate in its decision-making processes in a productive manner.

Further, emerging evidence indicates that public participation does, indeed, influence decision making and does not exist merely as an exercise in "participatory government." Additionally, evidence appears to indicate that participation in educational decision making has been sustained, allowing for a stronger, more informed, and more active public citizenry, lessening the likelihood for top-down imposition so often seen in other educational reform efforts, including those of the United States.[11]

Finally, the example of Finland, which will play a central role in the thesis of this work as it has many others, provides the clearest demonstration of how true decentralization (combined with a number of other imperative elements) can empower local governments and communities while maintaining an effective level of control and meaningful accountability. Also based largely out of a wide-scale rebuilding of its society after several years of entrenched autocratic and authoritative political rule, the people of Finland took a deep and earnest interest in creating a truly cohesive society based on trust and cooperation, of which the educational system played only a part in the overall reform efforts.

Unconvinced by the trend in the early 1990s to base education reform squarely within the context of neoliberal market theory, emphasizing private investment, test scores, and performance-based accountability that is decided and implemented in a top-down, corporate-style managerial context, Finland deliberately chose to focus instead on nurturing both the creativity and interest of its children, while fostering cultural respect for the expertise of teachers. Results of this approach has led to a complete decentralization of schooling in which not only local agencies, but in many cases individual teachers are entrusted with the task of choosing curriculum, devising and implementing creative pedagogical methodologies, evaluating their own students according to their own systems, and adjusting any of these elements at their discretion with little, if any, interference from an overarching educational management system.

Essentially, since all participants in the educational process are equally accountable but also free to perform their services in their chosen ways, a culture of collaboration, creative problem solving, and shared exploration has flourished. The elimination of high-stakes assessments, which are not used at all in primary or secondary school, and evaluation based on grading, which is prohibited after the fifth grade, has allowed teachers to remain focused on the one true concern, actual student learning, without the distraction or threat of punitive evaluative processes that have little to do with classroom practice or pedagogy anyhow.[12]

Decentralization takes a relatively clear form within the Finnish conceptualization. First, the focus of the Finnish curriculum is on flexibility and somewhat flexible standards. Because pedagogical methodologies, content, and evaluation procedures are not imposed upon Finnish teachers but rather chosen by them, teachers are able to build on existing practices that have been effective and to experiment with innovations on these practices without the threat of punitive evaluation for "failure" in either an individual or collaborative context.

Second, Finnish teachers are encouraged to focus on both broad and deep learning combined with creativity. This allows the teacher latitude to focus on various aspects of the individual's development including personality, morality, creativity, and academic skills, while maintaining individual student interest as the focal point of such learning.

Finally, without the imposition of decontextualized, standardized high-stakes testing efforts to account for "student achievement," Finnish teachers are trusted to determine contextual methods of assessment and evaluation of student learning that are meaningful to them and their students, reporting the results in ways that are meaningful and directly relevant to the curriculum and pedagogical practices.

Indeed, it would be easy to level the argument that the Finnish education system is set up to reward itself by its lack of "quantifiable" accountability methods, creating, essentially, a self-serving system that does not truly engage in evaluation and can therefore claim success in absence of any other "proof." However, as Finland is a member of the Organisation for Economic Cooperation and Development (OECD), it has participated and ranked in top positions in the international Programme for International Student Assessment (PISA), the results of which are most often cited by educational reformers in the United States.

In most cases, according to the rhetoric, the poor results of the United States on the PISA assessment certify its school systems' failure and legitimize the use of standardized reform practices. Furthermore, while the diagnosis of anxiety-based mental illness and mood disorders, as well as school phobia and disengagement appear to be increasing in the United States in direct correlation with current educational reforms, it remains minimal among Finnish students.[13–15]

The common thread that connects the successful decentralization strategies of Poland, India, and Finland is not so much the reform itself, but that the reform came, part and parcel, with greater social reform and focus on true democratic functioning. That is, while Poland, India, and Finland maintain a deep belief in the power of schools and schooling, they do not place the entire responsibility of social change on schools, as is the case in the United States.

In these countries' efforts, strengthening the role of the education system was an important component in a larger scale, nationally based cultural rejuvenation. Inherent in this effort was the deep realization of, respect for, and entwinement with cultural perspectives that are central to that country's ideologies, and using these cultural values to unify as opposed to divide. Indeed, from this perspective it is not necessary that cultures must hold identical value systems to create a successful education reform system. Rather, that each country is true to and inclusive of the inherent cultural representations it finds within its own culture and society, even if it is vastly heterogeneous.

Two clear examples are that of India and Finland, both of which continue to facilitate successful education reform from a decentralization perspective, but do so as an outgrowth of deeper national cultural and social change. From the Indian perspective, the cultural relevance of teacher thinking was held as a central component to the success of its education reform effort.

According to Clarke, the meaning of Indian education can be summarized by four main ideas: (1) a shared holistic worldview that regards individuals not as autonomous, but interconnected and interdependent, and creates a system in which social relationships is the driving force leading to cultural understanding, especially across cultures; (2) instruction as duty, or moral obligation, to help individuals know what they must or must not do as suggested by their culture; (3) structural hierarchy, in which Indian students display a sense of reverence, respect, and esteem toward their teacher as an expert, while the teacher displays a reciprocal sense of nurturing, responsibility, and empathy; and (4) the belief in collectively accumulated knowledge, indicating that individual choices should be steeped in collective conscious-ness rather than individual perception, experience, and benefit.

As such, the Indian teacher could not be said to be autonomous, but cen-ters his or her job in the main beliefs of the culture, using cultural relevance, rather than economic competitiveness, as its litmus for success.[16]

Finnish culture is, indeed, quite differently contextualized though no dif-ferent in its ability to reform its schooling practices in congruence with its cultural values, which are in line with overall governmental structure and the general functioning of the public sphere. According to Sahlberg:

> Education policies are necessarily interdependent on other social policies and on the overall political culture of a nation. The key success factor in Finland's development of a well-performing knowledge economy with good governance and a respected education system has been its ability to reach broad consensus on most major issues concerning future directions.[17]

Indeed, while many suggest that Finland is made up of a largely homoge-neous culture and, therefore, is not as challenged by ethnic diversity as other countries such as the United Kingdom and the United States, a number of studies indicate contrary findings, evidencing the increasing cultural diver-sity present in Finland without the economic stratification found elsewhere.[18] This is achieved by allowing equal access to roughly identical comprehensive schools regardless of socioeconomic standing, all of which are invested in equitably by the government.

Unification is further achieved by promoting an attitude of "loving learning," with success conceptualized as self-realization and socio-emotional growth instead of performance and achievement as measured by decontextualized standardized test scores. Finland centers its education philosophy on seven cor-nerstones: (1) holistic development of personality, which includes knowledge and skills, as well as creativity and interpersonal characteristics; (2) long-term visions of educational goals rather than short-term gains; (3) concentrating decision making at local and even individual teacher levels; (4) offering equal opportunity in schooling for all; (5) focusing on inclusive education for all chil-dren, focusing on creative approaches to classroom learning rather than adher-ence to superimposed standards; (6) belief in the leadership quality of younger, talented, and more "connected" school leaders with experience in education in order to ensure that innovation is informed by sound decision-making skills with over-imposing authority; and (7) focusing on conserving old, effective practices while allowing room for innovative ones, marked by acknowledg-ment and respect of teachers' wisdom, skill, and professionalism, and allowing them to learn from past experiences in a nonpunitive, reflective way.

It is clear that decentralization, if approached correctly and genuinely, can serve to empower both teachers and students leading to clear results in student learning while maintaining humanistic and individualistic approaches to pedagogy, as well as the values and virtues that are central to that specific culture. Those countries, like Poland, India, and Finland, which have appeared to struggle through and address the implementation challenges of decentralizing approaches, have been successful in both building conscious and well-prepared citizens who function in a larger context of community, as well as academically conscious and skillful members of a global society. These true successes, though perhaps less measurable by standardized tests and performance-based assessments, are likely to be shown as the cornerstone to these countries' continued economic, political, and cultural success.

NOTES

1. M. Fernanda Astiz, Alexander Wiseman, and David P. Baker. Slouching towards Decentralization: Consequences of Globalization for Curricular Control in National Education Systems. Comparative Education Review, 46(1), p. 66–88.
2. Carlos Ornelas (n.d.). The Politics of the Educational Decentralization in Mexico. Retrieved from http://citeseerx.ist.psu.edu/viewdoc/download?doi=10.1.1.2 02.5811&rep=rep1&type=pdf.
3. Ibid.
4. Bradley A. Levinson (May, 2014). Education Reform Sparks Teacher Protest in Mexico. Phi Delta Kappan, 48–51.
5. Ibid.
6. Tony Levitas and Jan Herczynski (2001). Decentralization, Local Governments, and Education Reform in Post-Communist Poland. Retrieved from https://www.rti.org/ pubs/levitas__LG__fiancne_reform_Poland.pdf.
7. Ibid.
8. Amanda Ripley. (2014). The Smartest Kids in the World: And How They Got That Way. New York: Simon & Schuster.
9. Mullikottu-Veettill and Mark Brady (2004). The Decentralisation of Education in Kerala State, India: Rhetoric and Reality. International Review of Education, 50, 223–243.
10. N.V. Varghese. (1996). Decentralisation of Educational Planning in India: The Case of the District Primary Education Programme. International Journal of Educational Development, 16 no. 4, 355–365.
11. Patrick Heller, K. N. Harilal, and Shubdam Chaudhuri. (2007). Building Local Democracy: Evaluating the Impact of Decentralization in Kerala, India. World Development, 35 no. 4, 626–648.
12. Pasi Sahlberg (2007). Education Policies for Raising Student Learning: The Finnish Approach. Journal of Education Policy, 22 no. 2, 147–171.
13. Ibid.
14. Douglas C. Wren & Jeri Bensen (2004). Measuring Test Anxiety in Children: Scale Development and Internal Construct Validation. Anxiety, Stress, & Coping, 17 no. 3, 227–240.

15. Nathaniel von der Embse, Justin Barterian, and Natasha Segool. (2013). Test Anxiety Interventions for Children and Adolescents: A Systematic Review of Treatment Studies from 2000-2010. Psychology in the Schools, 50 no. 1, 57–71.

16. Prema Clarke (2003). Culture and Classroom Reform: The Case of the District Primary Education Project, India. Comparative Education, 39 no. 1, 27–44.

17. Sahlberg, 2007, p. 166

18. Sahlberg, 2007.

Chapter 7

Real Value Added

Respecting Teachers and Educationists in Education Reform Policy

In many countries' efforts toward attaining the true decentralization of public schooling, the input of both active teachers and educationists (such as professors of education, researchers, and other relevant public intellectuals) is taken seriously and applied to the actual development of the various education reform policies drafted. While approached in a number of different ways, it is clear that teachers' perceptions and ideas are highly valued in the policymaking process in countries such as New Zealand, Poland, and Finland.

Contrarily, while the specter of teacher participation is ever-present in rhetoric and even some "official" documents of education reform in the United States, there is little, if any, actual representation or serious consideration given to those who are actively teaching in American classrooms. In some cases, such perspectives are even derided should they break from the current political thrust or imply ideas that are seen as sympathetic to a "teacher union" mentality.

The massive effort of the Common Core State Standards (CCSS) project, which can very well be equated to current education reform in the United States, is a prime example. As both its verbiage and its resultant "mandates" in the area of assessment became nearly universal in implementation in the United States, as well as its adoption being virtually mandatory for consideration as a recipient of Race to the Top funds, the CCSS initiative has been a central mechanism to the widespread education reform of the twenty-first century.

Much scuttlebutt has been present regarding whether teachers had an active role in the drafting and finalization of the standards themselves, and all sides are adamant in holding rigidly to their own conclusions. Indeed, there are a number of organizations and individuals who suggest that their influence was directly significant to the drafting and publishing of the standards.[1,2]

However, far more significant than the input and feedback process is the governance structure of the standard-issuing process itself. That is, who truly held the "power" for final decision making? From this perspective, the answer is quite clear.

In 2009, the names of participants in the principal "work groups" responsible for drafting the verbiage of the English Language Arts and Mathematics Common Core State Standards were released by the National Governors Association (NGA) and the Council of Chief State School Officers (CCSO), the cosponsors of the Common Core initiative. Though this was the extent to which the public would have any knowledge of its workings. As suggested by the press release:

> The work group's deliberations will be confidential throughout the process. States and national education organizations will have the opportunity to review and provide evidence-based feedback on the draft documents throughout the process.[3]

A close look at the composition of both work groups reveals an interesting though unsurprising bias in membership. In the Mathematics Work Group, 14 of the 15 members were directly associated with either Achieve Inc., the aforementioned corporate-connected not-for-profit organization which now functions largely as a Washington DC-based think tank and has strong ties to the educational testing industry going back decades, or a selection of other powerful organizations from within the testing industry, including ACT, Inc. and the College Board. For the English Language Arts (ELA) group, the same is true regarding 11 out of the 14 members.[4]

Even at the surface level the dubiousness of this consortium is made apparent. However, deeper analysis reveals that the vast majority of the participants have never taught in the classroom, and those who had were either associated with other content areas apart from the group with which they were associated, or were out of the classroom for several years.[5]

While this is the case for the work groups, there was also an additional consortium branded as the "feedback group." Indeed, for this group, the members were comprised more largely of educationists (mostly college professors) and a scarce number of public school teachers (one middle school mathematics teacher from Virginia and one "Instructional Performance Coach" from a charter school in Washington, DC). However, the largely insignificant function of this "feedback" group was clear from the outset:

> The role of the feedback group is to provide information backed by research to inform the standards development process by offering expert input on *draft* [italics added] documents. Final decisions regarding the common core standards document will be made by the Standards Development Work Group. The Feedback group will play an *advisory* [italics added] role, not a *decision-making* [italics added] role.

Clearly the standard drafting process was an endeavor that was to be shared with only those who were chosen directly by the NGA and the CCSO, whose preference for corporate input and away from teacher expertise was unequivocal.[6] The public, save perhaps for those carefully chosen token representatives, were generally left out of the process which likely affected the adoption process at both national and state levels.[7,8,9]

Efforts like this, however, are not ubiquitous internationally. While much of the education reform in New Zealand (under the moniker National Certificate in Educational Achievement, or NCEA) took on an earlier form of neoliberal overhauling and focus on criterion-referenced assessment, current efforts appear to be focusing more directly on teacher expertise, and the ability for teachers to direct enrichment and professional development opportunities on their own.

Drawing largely on the idea that teacher education and professional development during an education reform phase for practicing teachers is vastly different than that of initial or preservice teacher training, teachers themselves are being enabled to play a more active and direct role in determining topics and areas for their own further professional development, with variability permitted between schools. As such, teachers and administrators are respected as those who are best qualified to determine how individual funds are to be spent in order to target the professional development needs for their own student body.

Indeed, research is beginning to show that the new emphasis on providing decision latitude directly to teachers rather than dictating it from a centralized locus is indicative of higher satisfaction among teachers. This allows them to be more sensitive to and accepting of large-scale education reform efforts.[10]

Education reform efforts in Poland have also sought to actively include teachers in the policymaking process. During its transition from being a centralized government to one which empowered more local decision-making bodies, councils were formed to oversee the hiring and maintenance of school directors. These local councils would be responsible for electing specific directors for a five-year term. The councils were, by design, representative of multiple facets of the community that the school served, including teachers, parents, and local governments, among other groups receiving the right to name two members to the committee. This process maximized equal representation for each group, despite their specific interest, in the decision-making councils by devising an infrastructure for change that was far more representative of local concerns.[11]

Similarly to the overall decentralization effort, a key of which is empowering local teachers to make curricular decisions, the Ministry of Education in Poland permitted individual teachers to choose among certified textbooks. Though it is important to note that this was not indicative of total freedom, but only of choice among a controlled set of materials, it is indicative of increased choice and an acceptance of nonuniversality in curriculum selection and an increasing respect for the value of individual teacher expertise.

An important outgrowth of this new respect for teachers and their expertise resulted in a specialist-based evaluation system, within which teachers are not evaluated based on decontextualized test scores or potentially biased supervisor observations, but rather on a coordinated and systematic decision-making process. This process is facilitated by an independent committee that is comprised of education specialists who will determine the teacher's promotion through a relatively simple four-step pay grade system.[12]

Perhaps the best example of social valuation of teachers is found in Finland's system. Endemic to the education system itself is the culture of trust carefully and earnestly nurtured throughout Finnish society. Finland's approach to teachers and teaching can be described as

> encouraging teachers and students to try new ideas and methods, learn about and through innovations, and cultivate creativity in schools, while respecting schools' pedagogic legacies . . ..What is important is that Finnish education policies today are a result of four decades of systematic, mostly intentional development that has created a culture of diversity, trust, and respect within Finnish society in general and within its education system in particular.[13]

Part of this effort's success and its resulting trust in teachers as education experts is Finland's national attention to governing by consensus; an element which has positioned the Teachers' Trade Union as a respected and valued player in negotiating educational reform, especially in the area of resisting neoliberal competitive approaches.[14] This is in stark contrast with the deep neoliberal and conservative distrust, if not outright disdain, for teachers' unions in the United States; opposition to which is often lauded in elected officials and seen as a requisite to true education reform.

A main result of Finland's culture of trust is the respect for not only teachers' professional expertise, but also respecting their autonomy as an integral part of the teaching, learning, and creative process. One component of this approach is the absence of compulsory in-service trainings determined in a top-down manner. Rather, teachers and schools are responsible for directing and organizing their own forms of professional development, similar to the system emerging in New Zealand. The perception of the teaching profession in Finland has therefore flourished:

> Today the Finnish teaching profession is on par with other professional workers; teachers can diagnose problems in their classrooms and schools, apply evidence-based and often alternative solutions to them and evaluate and analyze the impact of implemented procedures [themselves]. Parents trust teachers who know what is best for their children.[15]

Indeed, research supports the evidence of widespread respect of teachers by parents as well as the greater community, as they are generally seen as integral members of a healthy civil society and builders of a strong future.[16]

But what is more important than a culture of trust and the granting of teacher autonomy to practice is the active role that teachers played (and continue to play) in the very designing of educational policies and practices. Coming off of a highly centralized governmental system, Finnish society took an active and earnest role in establishing a trust-based civil system in their country throughout the 1990s. Part of this new system was an increased faith in the schools as integral in the propagation and maintenance of the new culture. But this newly infused belief was placed upon teachers and administrators with trust, and not based on punitive and consequence-driven policies that placed more attention on failure rather than success:

> Inviting teachers and principals to participate in school development had an enormously positive impact on the Finnish education sector. . . . Teachers could see that the system believed that schools and communities are the places where decisions concerning curriculum and overall arrangement of schooling should be made. . . . Schools very quickly embraced their new roles in leading change within this culture of trust. . . . Each school, at least in theory, could design its own change strategy with mission statements, vision and implementation methodologies, and schedules. This dimension of trust has played the most significant role in propelling Finland's education system past those of many other nations.[17]

These reforms were made possible by the attention that was paid not only to economic importance, managerial responsibility, and accountability, but also to shifting and improving the very paradigms that guided school functioning and teaching practices. Reforms from this perspective focused on building a new culture that would lead to better schools, rather than expecting a new educational system to be responsible for building the new culture. This characterization is made clear in that

> Finland's high achievement seems to be attributable to a whole network of inter-related factors in which students' own areas of interest and leisure activities, the learning opportunities provided by school, parental support and involvement as well as social and cultural context of learning and of the entire education system combine with each other.[18]

Telling in this emphasis on culture and not only academic achievement and economic competitiveness is Finland's status as being one of the most significant producers of musicians of any other country, a fact in which the country takes deep pride.[19]

But perhaps the most important by-product of this wide-scale and systematic focus on teacher and educationist expertise is the general support and sense of progress in Finnish education reform, a reality that cannot be declared about the United States or Mexico, both of whom have focused their education reform efforts largely on neoliberal economic philosophy and accountability-based procedures which are largely, if not entirely, punitive.

Instead, Finnish teachers appear to view the focus of education reform in Finland as an effort to increase cooperation and collaboration between multiple players in civil society, all of whom are respected as influential. Some studies suggest up to 80 percent of Finnish teachers reporting high levels of job satisfaction, and others suggest nearly all Finnish teachers support the country's education reform policies, a stark contrast to that of the United States.[20] The following is a concise summary of the success of Finnish education reform as it relates to teacher respect and autonomy:

> Popular teachers came to be very highly trained. Except for during the transition period the relationship between the State and the teachers' union (OAJ) developed well, especially in international comparison. Strike activities have been scarce, and the Comprehensive School Reform increased the teacher's status in society and influence on education policy. More than ever, teachers became a trustworthy ally of the state, members of the cultural and economic elite. What is more, people have been awakened to the fact that it is only through education that it is possible to climb the social ladder, or even to keep up one's position. Teachers have become judges in terms of determining the directions of our children's future. This right has been handed over to them by the state from above and by parents from below.[21]

Indeed, without widespread and truly legitimate valuation of teachers and their professional expertise, true education reform will remain impossible. It is clear that an element of a truly decentralized system of education is the legitimization of teachers and educationists as qualified professionals, if not experts, and their positive regard as not only contributors, but as shapers of society and culture in both the present and the future.

While there can be little argument that the culture of trust that has been achieved in Finland is far from being a reality in the United States, a shift in trust to teachers themselves as responsible for their students' learning in the absence of an imposing and decontextualized oversight from those who are entirely detached from the true profession is imperative. This may be the point at which a culture of trust could begin to be facilitated in the United States. The social importance of school and its purpose is clearly respected; the society must now imbue the same trust in its teachers to teach as it does in its doctors to cure.

NOTES

1. Jeffrey S. Solochek (October 21, 2013). "Teachers Were Not Involved in the Common Core State Standards, Say Common Core Opponents." http://www.politifact.com/florida/statements/2013/oct/21/public-comments-common-core-hearing/teachers-were-not-involved-developing-common-core-/.

2. http://www.nea.org/home/46665.htm.

3. http://www.nga.org/cms/home/news-room/news-releases/page_2009/col2-content/main-content-list/title_common-core-state-standards-development-work-group-and-feedback-group-announced.html.

4. Ibid.

5. Mercedes Schneider (April 23, 2014). Those 24 Common Core Work Group Members. https://deutsch29.wordpress.com/2014/04/23/those-24-common-core-2009-work-group-members/.

6. Mercedes Schneider (April 25, 2014). A Tale of Two NGA Press Releases, and Then Some. https://deutsch29.wordpress.com/2014/04/25/a-tale-of-two-nga-press-releases-and-then-some/.

7. Susan Ohanian, "28 Questions About the Common Core" Retrieved from http://vtdigger.org/2013/08/13/ohanian-28-questions-about-the-common-core/.

8. NYS Allies for Public Education. Retrieved from http://www.nysape.org/allies.html.

9. Texas Freedom Network. Retrieved from http://tfn.org/issue/education/ .

10. Louise Starkey, Anne Yates, Luanna H. Meyer, Cedric Hall, Mike Taylor, Susan Stevens, and Rawiri Toia. "Professional Development Design: Embedding Educational Reform in New Zealand." *Teaching and Teacher Education*, 25, 181–189, (2009).

11. Tony Levitas and Jan Herczynski. (2001). Decentralization, Local Governments, and Education Reform in Post-Communist Poland. https://www.rti.org/pubs/levitas_LG_finance_reform_Poland.pdf.

12. Ibid.

13. Pasi Sahlberg. "Education Policies for Raising Student Learning: The Finnish Approach." *Journal of Education Policy*, 22 no. 2, (2007), 147–171.

14. Ibid.

15. Ibid., p. 152

16. Hannu Simola. "The Finnish Miracle of PISA: Historical and Sociological Remarks on Teaching and Teacher Education." *Comparative Education*, 41 no. 4, (2005), 455–470.

17. Sahlberg, "Education Policies," 2007, p. 157.

18. Jouni Valijarvi, Pirjo Linnakyla, Pekka Kupari, Pasi Reinikainen, and Inga Arffman. (2002). Finnish Success in PISA. Some Reasons Behind It. (Jyvaskyla, Institute for Educational Research, University of Jyvakyla), 46.

19. Sahlberg, "Education Policies," 2007.

20. Simola, "The Finnish Miracle," 2005.

21. Risto Rinne, as cited by Simola, "The Finnish Miracle," 2005.

Chapter 8

Appreciation, Education, Innovation
The Finnish Example of Teacher Education

The challenge of how to best educate and prepare preservice teachers, or teachers not yet active in the classroom, has become part and parcel with the greater discussion of education reform. Indeed, one notion with which virtually all factions concur is that the education program intended to prepare teachers to be educators themselves is an indispensable facet of an effective school system. Differences in the perspectives, opinions, and foundations of such education become quite clear, however, when it comes to determining how, why, by whom, and to what degree preservice teachers should be educated and trained before they are deemed prepared for genuine classroom practice.

Indeed, the extant literature over the last two decades has experienced a demonstrative increase in attention toward the issue of teacher preparation in educational policy and its related policy documents internationally.[1] This is highly indicative of the central role that teachers are seen to play in the educational and, by extension, economic and social prosperity of a country. As the Organisation for Economic Cooperation and Development (OECD) purports:

> All countries are seeking to improve their schools and to respond better to higher social and economic expectations. As the most significant and costly resource in schools, teachers are central to school improvement efforts. Improving the efficiency and equity of schooling depends, in large measure, on ensuring that competent people want to work as teachers, their teaching is of high quality and that all students have access to high quality teaching.[2]

As one of the main thrusts for education reform is framed within the context of neoliberalism and its corresponding standards and achievement-based performance, it stands to reason that many of the discussions around teacher

59

preparation adopt and apply the same framework. That is, if the purpose of education is to facilitate global competitiveness for students, then the onus for attaining "world-class" standards is superimposed on teachers and teacher candidates. While proponents of a neoliberal perspective of education reform would aptly champion this perspective, many do not, and some even take distinct offense at the notion that good teaching is operational, measurable, and quantitatively relevant. As Furlong, Cochran-Smith, and Brennan suggest:

> The [neoliberal] reasoning behind these [quantitative] arguments . . . is at best overstated and at worst, quite faulty. Critics in a variety of countries have questioned whether education alone can create (or negate) the economic well-being of a nation, and whether the quality of teaching and teachers is the overwhelming factor in raising educational outcomes. Despite these and other quite legitimate questions, a new national preoccupation with the supply and quality of teachers is now almost universal and, encouraged by organizations such as the OECD and the World Bank.[3]

Many facets currently have an influence on the workings of teacher education and preparation, including higher education councils, accreditation agencies, professional organizations, and individual faculties of colleges and universities. The ultimate question remains, however, as to which facet(s) should and will retain control over the teacher education process. This is a virtual mirror of the central question of ownership in public schools.

It is not surprising, however, that given the success of the Finnish education system in both student performance and contentedness, social and parental trust, and the generally high level of job satisfaction, that the corresponding teacher preparation system is exemplary, yet quite different from that of many others' approaches, namely, the United States. Indeed, the model of teacher education follows in very much the same vein as their overall philosophy of education reform: building a sense of autonomy, professionalism, reflection, content knowledge, and creativity. The Common European Principles for Teacher Competences and Qualification, published in 2005, echoes this notion in its suggestion that

> the teaching profession [is] a graduate and multidisciplinary profession. Furthermore . . . teacher education has to guarantee that teachers have knowledge of the subject matter and of pedagogy, the skills and competences to guide and support learners, and an understanding of the social and cultural dimensions of education.[4]

Finland's interpretation of this conceptualization was to prepare their teachers in the broadest sense—that is, to be able to be mindful and attend to their students' socio-emotional growth above all, and to have pedagogical knowledge and attitudes that are supported by the latest research.[5]

Regarding teaching as multidisciplinary, teacher education programs, which are initiated at the bachelor's degree level and continue through to a master's degree level (as a mandate), encompass a broad range of subjects such as didactics, educational psychology, sociology of education, philosophy of education, and history of education, which are included to facilitate not only the pedagogical processes, but also the foundational and functional purposes of education itself. Focus on rigorous but meaningful and deep study from a holistic perspective, rather than from a strictly performance and content-based "competency" perspective, has become a hallmark of Finnish teacher education.

Because of this deep appreciation for the comprehensiveness of teaching, Finnish teachers, when they have completed their studies, are respected, well regarded, and trusted as autonomous professionals and experts, and are permitted and encouraged to implement their own forms of instruction, innovation, and evaluation of their students based directly on their expertise.[6] As suggested by Heidi Krzywacki, a Finnish teacher educator at the University of Helsinki, "[W]hen you get your first job, nobody ever enters your classroom to see how you're doing. There is no tutor, no mentor. You just start working."[7]

The approach of trust-based evaluation of teachers and teacher candidates in Finland also encompasses the means of evaluation within the teacher education program. While it is important to note that the entrance requirements to teacher education programs in Finland are very rigorous, universities do not base their selection of teaching candidates, which comprise only about 10 percent of the applicants, on academic credentials, scholastic aptitude, and achievement alone. Indeed, some of the most scholastically apt students are rejected for entrance into teacher education programs in Finland. Instead, applicants who are seen as being multifaceted, passionate, and have natural leadership capabilities like musicians, athletes, and community activists are more likely to be chosen.[8]

This theory behind this type of selection process is, indeed, grounded in research as indicated by a number of studies which show that noncertified teachers from Teach for America, who are often from the nation's top colleges, are less effective than traditionally trained and certified teachers.[9,10] That is, academic prowess is not associated with more effective teaching, regardless of content focus.

A practical application of trust-based assessment is Finland's increasing use of portfolios for teacher candidates, a trend that is growing in Europe as a whole. This shift in evaluative perspective represents a greater difference in

paradigm; one that regards summative assessment practices in higher education as being most informed by traditional performance-based methods to a
formative one that will more accurately demonstrate a teacher candidate's
learning and development over time. This approach allows the student to take
a more active and reflective role in his or her own development as a teacher,
and learn to self-assess in a way that is truly applicable and practical in a
genuine classroom environment.

Such a formative and deeply reflective type of assessment is regarded
as far more representative of the deep and complex processes involved in
teaching and the active development as a teacher. Rather than distilling such
a multifaceted endeavor such as teaching into a decontextualized score on a
performance-based assessment that has little relevance to classroom practice
or student learning, approaching assessment from a teacher-based, metacog-
nitive approach is vastly more holistic and comprehensive.[11]

It is important to note that portfolios are not only self-assessed in Finland,
but also evaluated by teacher educators throughout the entire teacher preparation process. Rather than positioning itself as a punitive-based, capstone type
of exercise in accountability that comes as a culminating activity at the end
of a teacher preparation program (as the approach in the United States can
be accurately characterized), the evaluative process entwined in the portfolio
context is both an example of and an instructive exercise in the dynamic, dialogic, and interactive process of meaningful evaluation. Therefore, it is one
that the teacher candidate him-or herself may use with their own students one
day. Moore and Ashe suggest that

> despite an appreciation on the part of beginning teachers of the potential
> value of reflective practice, many new teachers choose not to reflect on their
> practice constructively and critically, preferring to fall back on pre-conceived
> understandings of how they and their pupils should conduct themselves in the
> classroom.[12]

Deeply engaging in the reflective and dialogic process of meaningful
evaluation will allow the teacher candidate to directly experience the value of
the process itself, thus lessening the likelihood of becoming "traditionalized"
in his or her own classroom practice. This holistic approach to teacher education is often categorized under the moniker of "research-based teacher education."[13] While the use of the terms "research-based" or "evidence-based" is
evoked almost incessantly in discussions of education and education reform,
its connotation, and even denotation, in the Finnish context is diametrically
opposed to that of the American, or perhaps greater positivist, context.

While in the American context, the concept of evidence-basis is often
reduced to a particular instructional methodology's presence and validation

in the professional empirical literature in a decontextualized manner, the Finnish conceptualization is based on four main characteristics.[14]

The first concept is regarding teaching according to systematic analysis. That is, teaching is to be seen as both a science and an art, and it is up to the teacher preparation program to instill in the candidate the ability to decipher the two aspects.

The second concept is that all teaching should be based on research, meaning an earnest, deep, and reflective investigation of the practices a teacher plans to employ which may be informed by empirical-based research, but also by strong theoretical and philosophical foundations.

The third concept is that educational activities are to be organized in a manner that requires the teacher candidate to utilize and develop skills of argumentation, decision making, and justification for using such techniques in order to address pedagogical issues and student learning.

The final component is that the students themselves learn academic research skills in order to become better consumers, producers, and utilizers of research-based information in their own teaching.[15]

As summated by two prominent Finnish education researchers:

> Ultimately, the goal of research-based teacher education is pedagogically-thinking, reflective and inquiry-oriented teachers. This means that the purpose is not to educate researchers or even teacher-researchers *per se*. The objective is to acquire an inquiring attitude to teaching. Thus, teachers are able to observe, analyze, and develop their work. Teachers' pedagogical thinking means the ability to conceptualize everyday phenomena, to look at them as part of a larger instructional process and to justify decisions and actions made during this process.[16]

Indeed, it would not be fair to suggest that the elements highlighted in the Finnish approach to teacher education are not also deeply entwined in that of American teacher education. They are, in fact, quite present. This presence, then, comes to serve the most important point regarding the difference between the guiding foundations of teacher education and preparation in Finland and that in the United States.

Teacher educators, the school of education faculty members, and a number of other professional stakeholders in teacher education in the United States have all designed teacher education programs at their respective institutions in a very similar manner to that of the Finnish. Essentially, in many respects existing programs have been designed in the correct way, it is the superimposition of decontextualized accountability practices that have been detrimental.

It is nearly impossible to find teacher education programs that do not have, as its very foundations, the notions of diversity, pedagogy, problem solving, critical thinking, research, dialectics, philosophy, and social justice interweaved throughout its courses. This is so because the designers of such programs are, for the most part, educators or educationists in one way or another. Should the American social order respect the autonomy of teachers and instill the same level of trust in them as in Finland, it is likely that our school system would reach the same capacity and hold the same value as it does in Finland.

However, this is, quite sadly, not the case. The regard for American teachers, by both large factions of the general public as well as a considerable, if not overwhelming body of policymakers, legislators and politicians is quite the opposite: it is one of deep suspicion, disrespect, and punishment for perceived "failure."

Consider one project in the recent policy innovations of the United States—the emergence of the Teacher Performance Assessment (edTPA), a portfolio-based assessment of teacher candidates seeking state certification. According to its official website,

> edTPA is a performance-based, subject-specific assessment and support system used by teacher preparation programs throughout the United States to emphasize, measure, and support the skills and knowledge that all teachers need from Day 1 in the classroom. . . . The assessment features a common architecture focused on three tasks: Planning, Instruction, and Assessment. . . . Aspiring teachers must prepare a portfolio of materials during their student teaching clinical experience. . . . edTPA builds on decades of teacher performance assessment development and research regarding teaching skills and practices that improve student learning.[17]

The decades of research is attributed to the initial project established at Stanford Center for Assessment, Learning, and Equity (SCALE), an institute at Stanford University's School of Education whose members created and piloted research that led to the development of edTPA. At the surface level, this plan appears to be innocuous, as much of the current educational reform rhetoric does, especially when it is presented as a "portfolio-based assessment" which, as demonstrated before, has been shown to be successful in Europe. This putative innocuousness begs the question: What informed stakeholder would be opposed to such a process, especially if it is portfolio-based and results in higher quality teaching?

The problem here is no different than the last instance for which this question was posed. This process, though cloaked in the socially significant issue of teacher quality has become ensconced in the same privatization takeover involving one of the main players: Pearson, Inc. While many of the problematic features of the scoring process for edTPA, which is entirely outsourced, designed, and managed by Pearson are camouflaged by the qualification that the scorers of the edTPA are current or retired education professionals (which, indeed, they are), these scorers do not use their own sense of evaluation and expertise to evaluate the portfolios, but rather do so based on a multi-hour, rubric-based training provided by Pearson.[18,19] That is, they are not independent scorers, they are contracted scorers obligated to adhere to prescribed rubrics.

Therefore, the entire evaluation process is facilitated externally to the teacher candidate's education program, furthering the erroneous assumption that *all* teacher programs should be expected to meet the same "rigorous" standards for teacher preparation, regardless of programmatic philosophies, approaches, and means of instruction. Essentially, if teacher preparation programs are to produce teacher candidates that pass the edTPA, it is they who must conform to the dictated standards, not the "standards" which must conform to the expertise of teacher preparation program faculty.

Further, the process is deeply entrenched in profiteering, requiring prospective certified teachers to pay upwards of $300.00 for the edTPA evaluation itself, and an additional $100.00–$200.00 for either a reevaluation if particular sections are not passed or, as is the case in some states, an "alternative" pathway to attaining certification, such as passing an additional test in place of resubmitting the edTPA portfolio, which also requires a fee.[20] As a result, scores of teacher candidates are required to pay, in even the best case scenario, well over $1,000.00 for additional certification requirements over and above that of their university program, and that is assuming that these measures are passed the first time. At least a sizeable portion of all of these proceeds goes to but one place: Pearson, Inc.

Equally concerning is the way in which the edTPA structures its portfolio construction and maintains the current emphasis on "scripting" teachers' interactions with their students. Indeed, if student teachers learn to teach using a script, the script becomes embedded and is propagated once he or she is a fully certified practicing teacher. Such scripting results not only in sterilized forms of portraying and providing information, but also sterilized forms of student engagement with such information.

Indeed, many of the components of edTPA are nearly identical in both content and engagement requirements to the quickly emerging standardized curricula materials adopted across a number of states that are based on the Common Core State Standards (CCSS).[21] As critical educator Wayne Au suggests of edTPA's effect on the teacher education program with which he is affiliated in Washington State:

> Without a doubt, edTPA is standardizing our teacher education program, and I'm not sure it has been for the better. In our teacher education program, an explicit politics of social justice is woven throughout most of our credential coursework. However, when we began looking at our student's edTPA . . . one

thing was striking: The political commitments of our teacher credential program were almost nowhere to be found within our students' work. Students who demonstrated explicit commitments to teaching for social justice in coursework and during student teaching, who saw curriculum and instruction as an important place to ask students to critically consider inequality and power, simply left their politics out of edTPA.[22]

Indeed, similar sentiments are expressed by teacher candidates themselves, especially those who have been taught, and have become personally dedicated, to the social justice basis of authentic teaching:

The edTPA forced me to address historical content in a specific, scripted way. It was difficult to teach authentically while adhering to the edTPA guidelines. Instead of planning my lessons as I would normally do, I had to repeatedly consult a 54-page handbook to make sure that I was following the script. . . . The prompts provided by Pearson did not allow me to fully express my teaching philosophy. In the three days I taught my edTPA learning segment, I lost a little of the joy that I found in teaching.[23]

The critical question when it comes to comparing the teacher education and preparation process in the United States with that of Finland and other educationally progressive countries comes down to one main question: What is the difference? The answer to this is quite clear. Finnish teachers, once they have graduated and been deemed ready by the experts in their teacher preparation program, are not required to prove themselves any farther. They enter the classroom, function autonomously out of a deep obligation to their calling as teachers, and are trusted to do what they were trained to do without incessant punitive oversight cloaked as "accountability." They need not prove themselves further to a privately managed body of assessors, nor do they need to incur additional exorbitant personal costs to engage in superfluous and largely invalid credentialing processes. Essentially, they are entwined in the greater trust-based society as prized contributors.

NOTES

1. John Furlong, Marilyn Cochran-Smith, and Marie Brennan. Policy and Politics in Teacher Education: International Perspectives. *Teachers and Teaching: Theory and Practice*, 14 no. 4, (2008), 265–269.

2. OECD (2005), 1.

3. Furlong et al., "Policy and Politics," 265.

4. European Commission (2005) as cited by Ritva Jakku-Sihvonen, Varpu Tissari, Aivar Ots, and Satu Uusiautti. "Teacher Education Curriculum after the Bologna Process—A Comparative Analysis of Written Curricula in Finland and Estonia." *Scandinavian Journal of Educational Research*, 56 no. 3, (2012), 261–275.

5. Jakku-Shivonen et al., "Teacher Education Curriculum."

6. Ibid.

7. Heidi Krzywacki (2009). "Becoming a Teacher: Emerging Teacher Identity in Mathematics Teacher Education." Retrieved from https://helda.helsinki.fi/bitstream/handle/10138/20029/becoming.pdf?sequence=1&origin=publication_detail.

8. Pasi Sahlberg (March 31, 2015). "Q: What Makes Finnish Teachers so Special? A: It's Not Brains." From http://www.theguardian.com/education/2015/mar/31/finnish-teachers-special-train-teach.

9. Linda Darling-Hammond, Deborah J. Holtzman, Su Jin Gatlin, and Julian Vasquez Heilig. "Does Teacher Preparation Matter? Evidence about Teacher Certification, Teach for America, and Teacher Effectiveness." *Educational Analysis Policy Archives,* 13 no. 42. From file:///C:/Users/eshyman/Downloads/147-436-1-PB.pdf.

10. Lackzo-Kerr, Ildiko. and Berliner, David C. (2002). "The Effectiveness of 'Teach for America' and Other Under-Certified Teachers on Student Academic Achievement: A Case of Harmful Public Policy." *Education Analysis Policy Archives,* 10 no. 37. From http://epaa.asu.edu/ojs/article/view/316/442.

11. Barry Groom and Irmeli Maunonen-Eskelinen. "The Use of Portfolios to Develop Reflective Practice in Teacher Training: A Comparative and Collaborative Approach between Two Teacher Training Providers in the UK and Finland." *Teaching in Higher Education,* 11 no. 3, (2006), 291–300.

12. Moore and Ashe, as cited by Groom and Maunonen-Eskelinen, "Use of Portfolios," 292.

13. Auli Toom, Heikki Kynaslahti, Leena Krokfors, Riitta Jyrhama, Reijo Byman, Katarina Stenberg, Katriina Maaranen, and Pertti Kansanen (2010). "Experiences of a Research-based Approach to Teacher Education: Suggestions and Future Policies." *European Journal of Education,* 45 no. 2, (2010), 331–344.

14. Ibid.

15. Ibid.

16. Ibid., 339

17. http://www.edtpa.com/PageView.aspx?f=GEN_AboutEdTPA.html.

18. edTPA Scoring FAQs. http://scoreedtpa.pearson.com/become-an-edtpa-scorer/edtpa-scorer-training-faqs.html.

19. Become an edTPA Scorer. http://scoreedtpa.pearson.com/become-an-edtpa-scorer.html.

20. http://www.highered.nysed.gov/tcert/certificate/certexamsedtpa.html.

21. http://www.pearsonschool.com/index.cfm?locator=PS2iJj&PMDbSiteId=2781&PMDbSolutionId=6724&PMDbSubSolutionId=&PMDbCategoryId=806&PMDbSubCategoryId=25741&PMDbSubjectAreaId=&PMDbProgramId=123401&elementType=correlations.

22. Wayne Au. "What's A Nice Test Like You Doing in a Place Like This? The edTPA and Corporate Education 'Reform.'" From http://www.rethinkingschools.org/archive/27)04/27_04_au.shtml.

23. Ibid.

Chapter 9

Power without Dominance

Governing Schools through Participatory Decision Making

The progression toward a more socially relevant, successful, and citizen-producing school system has been shown to be most effective and successful when implemented as part of a movement toward comprehensive social change. That is, identifying school systems as the main culprit for social and cultural degeneration of any type and, therefore, addressing such social problems only through schooling and school reform is not only a mistake, but also an experiment that is invariably bound for failure. The most likely course of effective reform is by targeting the greater social problems contemporaneously with the way in which those problems function within the school system itself, allowing for both greater social reform as well as educational reform.

In the United States, there is an ever-growing disparity between the "common" population (based largely on both economic class and race) and representation in government. That is, though the putatively democratic practice of "electing" officials is maintained, one's very ability to become an elected official (i.e., be financially stable and politically connected enough to maintain the finances for a continuous campaign) is based almost entirely on economic means and social connection, aspects of social mobility which are largely interdependent in American society. Complicating factors such as delegates and the antiquated system of the Electoral College also remain threats to direct representation and truly democratic processes.

As such, true representation of the greater population is decreasing exponentially. Furthermore, because of this disparity, the government's accountability to the common person is minimized, if not entirely negated. The popular vote is almost entirely ineffectual (as shown in *Gore v. Bush* 2000), and the corporate lobby seems to, for all intents and purposes, facilitate the general viability of successful political campaigns and, by extension, the happenings of government. Therefore, candidates feel little obligation toward their constituents, but rather to their donors, who are to ensure that their political longevity is maintained and mobilized across the political system. According to Narayan:

> From the perspectives of poor people worldwide, there is a crisis in governance. While the range of institutions that play important roles in poor people's lives is vast, poor people are excluded from participation in governance. State institutions are often neither responsive nor accountable to the poor [creating] little recourse to injustice, criminality, abuse and corruption by institutions, even though they still express their willingness to partner with them under fairer rules.[1]

The general result of such apathy and a feeling of malaise toward government and governance practices is the absence of participation and, ultimately, a complacence with a system that is designed to maintain oppression and promote collusion.[2] Maintenance of this trend is toxic, if not entirely fatal, to the practice of true democracy in terms of "governance by the people and for the people." In order to counter this widespread deleterious trend, a vast surge in participatory governance must be demanded and instituted by the common people (both poor and "middle class") in the United States as a reactive resistance. According to Gaventa, the necessity is

> to rebuild relationships between citizens and their local governments [which] means working both sides of the equation—that is, going beyond "civil society" or "state-based" approaches, to focus on their intersection, through new forms of participation, responsiveness and accountability. . . . The call for new forms of engagement between citizens and the state involves a reconceptualization of the meanings of participation and citizenship in relationship to democratic governance . . .. With the reconceptualization of participation as a right of citizenship, and with the extension of the rights to participation beyond traditional voting and political rights, comes the search for more participatory approaches to ensuring citizen voices in processes of democratic governance.[3]

Central to this idea is the revaluation of the role of citizenship among the people themselves. That is, it is not only essential that the common people insist on a movement toward reconceptualizing the governance structure itself from the top-down, but also inspire one another to cultivate a spirit of citizenship in which they regain their power. This power should not be to transpose the locus of dominance, but rather to truly engage in building a genuinely democratic, participatory system of governance that not only *represents* the people, but can be directly manipulated and affected *by* the people. This concept can be described as *integrative democratization,* which is the strategy [that] describes the relationship between individual actors and institutions . . . [in which] institutions are seen as a factor that shapes the very goals and perceptions of individuals . . . linked to the classical argument that people are not born as citizens . . . democracy must be learnt [*sic*] and this can be ensured only through relevant institutional frameworks that empower people by educating them.[4]

Thus, an analysis of power, and the institutions and relations of power between individuals themselves as well as between institutions and individuals is an imperative component to such a reconceptualization. Transformation in governance, especially one that involves a transfer of power from a small, concentrated elite faction to a more suffused, empowered public is one that must be proceeded with carefully, deliberately, and systematically. As Freire reminds us:

The oppressed, having internalized the image of the oppressor and adopted his guidelines, are fearful of freedom. Freedom would require them to eject this image and replace it with autonomy and responsibility. Freedom is acquired by conquest, not by gift. It must be pursued constantly and responsibly. Freedom is not an ideal located outside man; nor is it an idea which becomes myth. It is rather the indispensable condition for the quest for human completion.[5]

That is, freedom and power, though regained by conquest, must remain ethical, and its repossessors must deliberately act so as not to simply gain dominance, but to work, with great effort, to redistribute the power in the fair way that was originally sought.

Gaventa deepens the discussion by providing conceptualizations for three different "spaces" within which power can be found and utilized. *Closed spaces* are spaces in which the few privileged decision makers employ their power without consent or appeal to not only the public, but even other members of the governmental system.

Invited spaces are spaces into which particular individuals, be they representatives, other elites, political allies, scholars, activists, or the like are asked to join to play a somewhat participatory role, however limited. Within these spaces participation from the public is widened, yet still tightly controlled and deliberate as such participation is limited only to those who have been permitted entry.

Finally, *claimed/created spaces* are those which are either taken or created autonomously by less powerful actors enacted as power sources from or toward the dominant actors. Grassroots movements or activist committees that formed of their own volition and insist on representation through action represent common forms of these spaces.

Perhaps the most common and relatively successful experiment in participatory government has been that of participatory budgeting. The concept of participatory budgeting allows the citizens themselves to determine how certain percentages of a budget are spent by public institutions. While there a variety of means by which participatory budgeting can be facilitated, some less direct, such as those via representative councils that use citizens' votes as "advisory," while others, more direct, which give citizens direct channels to public spending, the movement toward such direct participation in as fundamental a government process as spending public money is heartening and promising for the future success of a fully participatory government.

West Bengal and Kerala, India, for example, have created both representative and direct channels for spending public monies as well as developing additional capital to individual villages. Porto Alegre, Brazil, largely seen as the originator of such participatory budgeting practices, enables its residents to directly make budgeting choices to use monies toward betterment projects such as road construction and improvement, electricity access, and various other local amelioration projects.[6]

Indeed, there are also elements of similar projects in the United States. Chicago residents led a catalyzing repossession of many aspects of its policing and educational institutions, giving an unprecedented level of power to local residents. The Wisconsin Regional Training Partnership is an effort that has united organized labor unions, groups of corporate management teams, and government officials to target transparency in employment practices including transitions, career planning, and equity focused training opportunities.[7,8]

How, then, are these notions of participatory governance to work within school reform itself? First, it must be recapitulated that school reform, in the absence of greater social reform, is not likely to be effective, especially when implemented in a top-down, authoritarian manner. Rather, larger scale social and cultural changes must be contemporaneously at work. The first step, then, is to determine a working definition:

> Governance is the process of policy making through active and cohesive discussion among policy makers who are interconnected through a broad range of networks. By its nature, governance is a multiple-stakeholder process and a function of the many ways that individuals and institutions, both public and private, manage their common affairs. This process includes actors beyond government, including market and civil society institutions.[9]

Government, if it is to be well structured, fair, and in service to the whole of the people must not be inequitably concentrated within a small group of decision makers, but able to be enacted upon by all of its multiple stakeholders. Essentially, power can be prevented from being overly concentrated by working more actively at localized rather than centralized levels, ensuring not only the meeting of needs of individual citizens, but the opportunity for these citizens to be actively engaged and participatory in the governing and acting process. The way in which this participatory system can be represented in the school can serve to redistribute the power to the local citizens and school participants as they, themselves, are not only a primary means of its financial support (through taxes and other fees), but because it is their very community which is being directly affected.

ESTABLISHMENT OF A COMMUNITY-BASED INTERDISCIPLINARY COUNCIL

One major means by which localized government can be empowered in the area of schooling is by reconceptualizing and redesigning both the constitution and the decision-making structure of the school board. In its current state (though there are, indeed, localized differences) the general model allows any taxpayer within that school district (or other designation of territory that shares a single school system) to be elected. Though this is, indeed, an action of democracy in that it is one of the few examples of truly accessible governance positions, it ever bears the risk of being comprised of individuals who lack expertise in any particular area that the school serves.

This system, in its current form, contributes to the widely held though deeply erroneous notion that schools are just like any other "system" needing good management techniques without the necessity of expertise in the area of learning, development, teaching and instruction, curriculum, language, special needs/disability, as well as a number of other specialized aspects of a school.

Composition of the Interdisciplinary Council

In order to counter this current system, which devalues the specialization needed to understand the specific functions of schools, a more deliberate interdisciplinary council that retains the electoral process would better serve the interests of both the school system itself, as well as the greater community. This council, whose specifics should be left up to the particular districts, should include multiple representatives of:

1. in-district teachers;
2. in-district school administrators;
3. independent/unaffiliated educationists (such as researchers, teacher education professors, authors, consultants, etc.);
4. in-district parents who represent *all* factions of children including the gifted and talented, general track/general education, students with mild

and moderate disabilities, students with severe and profound disabilities, English Language Learners of all linguistic denominations, as well as any other locally represented group;

5. students themselves representing a cross-section of demographics;
6. general community stakeholders including residents without children who are currently enrolled in the district's public schools, nonparent community members, local business owners, "general" taxpayers, and others who live in the community and contribute to the system in a variety of ways.

Governance Structure of Interdisciplinary Council and Community Participation

The interdisciplinary council, in this sense, will serve the same or, at least, similar type of role that previous school boards did, but will have a governance structure that is different with levels of decision-making latitude proportional not only to each group of members' *stake* in the community, but also to their expertise in the various areas of educational importance.

That is, while the specific number of representatives that comprise each subgroup of members should be left up to the individual districts (so that it may approach the decision-making process in the way that is best suited to the specific community), the preponderance of voting matters in the area of educational practice (i.e., curriculum choice, academic freedom, teacher evaluation, student assessment and evaluation, administrative evaluation, among others) will be left primarily to the teachers, with advisory roles played by the in-district administrators, independent educationists, in-district parents, and general community stakeholders. This preponderance of power allocated to the in-district teachers allows those who hold the true expertise as well as the means to administer such educational decisions to apply it in a meaningful, culturally relevant, socially relevant, and educationally relevant way.

Regarding fiduciary issues, which is an imperative of any oversight board of this magnitude, budgets should be handled in a pluralistic and participatory manner. Though such an endeavor is, indeed, an aspect that will require careful oversight, it is integral in the functioning of a truly democratic local government.

While the specific delineations should be determined by the interdisciplinary council itself, at least 20 percent of the budget must be allocated according to popular vote. Opportunities to vote, including building accessibility, universality of time allotment in which votes can be cast, ability for all to cast a vote by allowing multiple means of casting a vote (electronic, manual, verbal, etc.), and voting and voter oversight must be designed in a manner that is both fair and universal to all eligible community voters. The remaining percentage of the budget not accessible to the participatory community, accounting for nondiscretionary expenses, can be handled by the interdisciplinary council itself.

Interdisciplinary Council Oversight

In order to maximize transparency between the community and the interdisciplinary council, official communication of all types involving matters of the school district must be completely accessible to all community members. These forms of oversight must include (but may not be limited to):

1. sharing of e-mails and e-mail addresses to the public (for all correspondence carried out in the capacity of a council member);
2. open meetings that may be publicly attended or simulcast on the internet (recordings must also be made available to those without internet access through venues such as the public library, the public school administration center, or other publicly accessible buildings);
3. the opportunity for all members of the community to address all members of the council;
4. the obligation for all members of the council to respond to each individual correspondence when requested by the community member;
5. public access of all financial records;
6. the right for the community to elect for an independent audit of financial records in a given amount of time (to be determined by the council itself);
7. an oversight process that requires reporting to the state and federal educational agencies, but are not regulated by them;
8. By redistributing the power from centralized areas to local councils both the needs of the locality will be better met and the residents will be enabled to play a direct participatory role in governance process. Among the facilitation of need-meeting and resource-accessing, this genuine form of participation and control is apt to lead to a reinvigoration of truly democratic government as well as an enhanced faith in the democratic system, which has been shown to be eroding both nationally and internationally.[10] Reviving faith in a governance system is also likely to lead to a deeper sense of community membership for most (if not all) in the community by minimizing and, ultimately, eliminating marginalization of any kind.

NOTES

1. Deepa Narayan-Parker. *Crying Out for Change: Voices of the Poor* (Washington, DC: World Bank Publishers, 2000), 172.

2. John Gaventa (2004). "Towards a Participatory Governance: Assessing the Transformative Possibilities." In *Participation—From Tyranny to Transformation?: Exploring New Approaches to Participation in Development.* Samuel Hickey and Giles Mohan (Eds.). 25–39. Zed Books: London.

3. Ibid., 28.

4. Thomas Zittel and Dieter Fuchs. *Participatory Democracy and Political Participation: Can Participatory Engineering Bring Citizens Back in?* (New York: Routledge, 2006), 11.

5. Paulo Freire. *The Pedagogy of the Oppressed.* (New York: Bloomsbury, 1995), 47.

6. Archon Fung and Erik Olin Wright (2001). "Deepening Democracy: Innovations in Empowered Participatory Governance." *Politics & Society*, 29 no. 1, 5–41.

7. Ibid.

8. http://www.wrtp.org/.

9. Pan Suk Kim, John Halligan, Namshin Cho, Cheol H. Oh, and Angela M. Eikenberry. "Toward Participatory and Transparent Governance: Report on the Sixth Global Forum on Reinventing Government." *Public Administration Review*, 65 no. 6, (2005), 647.

10. Yves Cabannes, (2004). "Participatory Budgeting: A Significant Contribution to Participatory Democracy." *Environment & Urbanization*, 16 no. 1, (2004), 27–46.

Chapter 10

Let the Teachers Teach

Nurturing Respect and Trust for Teachers and the Teaching Profession

By looking deeply into the social contexts in which effective education reform has been fostered, especially that of Finland, an indelibly essential element to reform success is a genuine respect for and trust in teachers and the teaching profession. Perhaps no other profession in American society bears a more significant burden of responsibility combined with institutional and social mistrust than American teachers.

Not only are teachers held responsible for teaching children and young adults, they are held equally responsible for allaying virtually every cultural problem that exists in America through their teaching regardless of the accessibility, or lack thereof, of necessary resources; and while the expectations remain high, the support and the trust remain desperately low. This mistrust is epitomized by the current neoliberal system of accountability by which teachers' best case scenario is the avoiding of punishment, despite the system being touted as a meritocratic system that seeks to "reward" effective teachers.

A solid framework within which this perspective can be examined is that of organizational justice, which refers to individuals' perceptions of fairness present in the organizations within which they function.[1] Elements of such a concept include perceptions of equity, general sense of justice, participatory opportunities, treatment by colleagues and supervisors, consistency of leadership behavior, issues of subordination, corrective procedures for poor decision making, representation of all stakeholder parties, and a sense of morality and ethics.[2]

An essential element to organizational justice is the very real concept and application of trust. Indeed, though elusive to capture, there are a number of definitions proffered in the discourse. For now, the following conceptualization will be applied:

Trust is one party's willingness to be vulnerable to another party based on the confidence that the latter party is benevolent, reliable, competent, honest, and open.[3]

Trust in schools is essential because it involves all stakeholders within the educational system at all levels. While trust can exist between any combinations of parties, trust in the context of teachers is deemed as most important as it affects the very functioning of the classroom itself. Trust or mistrust can exist between teachers and community members, teachers and administrators, teachers and other teachers, teachers and parents, teachers and students, teachers and school board members, among other and even more complex permutations.

Further, in this vein, organizational trust can be viewed in two distinct contexts: institutional trust and relational trust. *Institutional trust* is the expectation of appropriate behavior within organized settings framed within the norms of that particular institution (e.g., schools are entrusted by parents to keep the needs of their children at highest priority). *Relational trust* is the result of repeated interactions between parties within the organization, leading to particular expectations of satisfaction or disappointment (e.g., a school district that repeatedly underservices children with disabilities will be expected to continue to do so, causing a negative perception of that school system for parents of children with disabilities).[4]

Unfortunately, research appears to be relatively clear that there is a commonality of mistrust, or even betrayal of trust, between American teachers and their respective administrators, which serves as a fundamental antagonist to any meaningful educational change. A clear and stark dichotomy is often in existence between teachers and administrators that is inherently inequitable, with administrators seen as the "decision makers" and teachers seen as the "rule followers," regardless of their participation in the decision-making process, which is often regarded as low if at all existent.[5] With most change regarded as initiated by the administrator (or policymaker), teachers are apt to continue to feel this sense of subordination, while also bearing the brunt of the burden and blame for its outcomes, especially if those outcomes are negative.

With a central tenet of the current argument founded upon decentralization, the importance of trust between local stakeholders and actors is regarded as the most important locus within which trust should be cultivated. As argued by a number of educationists, creating a productive, constructive, trusting, and supportive atmosphere at local levels within districts, buildings, grades, and individual classrooms is vastly more important in facilitating positive educational changes than top-down structural changes, especially when those changes are punitive in nature.[6] It is likely fair to say that virtually all top-down educational reforms in the United States have violated this concept, instilling instead an opposite system of suspicion, punishment, and disrespect in teachers' expertise and professional abilities.

Findings from studies examining the role of trust in teachers appear to be very clear. In one such study conducted in Finland and Estonia, roughly 600 mothers were surveyed regarding their trust in their children's teachers and schooling. While results indicate a generally high level of trust between mothers and teachers, findings also indicated that mothers were more trusting of teachers who viewed their teaching style as "child-centered" as opposed to "teacher-centered."[7]

The Finnish school system has, for several decades, built upon the concept of trust between parents and teachers, as well as between administrators and teachers. Such instances of trust are obvious in Finnish teachers' freedom to choose their own textbooks, topics for in-service training and professional development, school budgetary decisions, course offerings, and general teacher autonomy. Further, teachers are not evaluated by administrators using quantitative measures, nor are they expected to complete further qualification tasks beyond their teacher preparation programs' certification of their ability and competency as a teacher.

What then, must schools do, at the local level, to rebuild and then continue to foster a culture of trust? While these questions and reform efforts may not be divorced from the greater social efforts toward a more trusting society as well as a more transparent system of governance overall, there are a number of efforts that can be made to systematically shift public perception toward trust in teachers.

TEACHERS AS LEADERS WITH REAL DECISION LATITUDE

The previous chapter delineated a reformed system of school governance, with fundamental decision latitude relegated to a council, though checked by mandatory participatory opportunities for general community members and taxpayers. However, a clear stipulation was made that educational decisions will be made, primarily, by in-district teachers. Such a system can only work if there is a corresponding and genuine deep trust in the expertise of teachers.

State education departments must begin by eliminating, or at least minimizing the number of post-curricular requirements for teachers to complete before being deemed "certified" and thus prepared to teach in their selected area of preparation. In this sense, states may maintain the concept of state certification, but should grant this qualification based on the discretion and recommendation of specific colleges of teacher education, not decontextualized and profit-driven standardized testing requirements required beyond the college degree (as an example, teachers in New York State are required to take upwards of three tests in addition to the edTPA portfolio in order to become certified[8]).

Second, the system of in-service and professional development require-ments must be revised with teachers at the helm of content-based decision making. That is, teachers should, indeed, be required to continue to take in-service workshops and engage in various types of professional development over the course of their entire career. But the teachers themselves should be granted the decision latitude to determine what topics or in what areas they need training and deeper education.

Teachers must also be given the opportunity to choose from what providers these professional development endeavors will come. In this sense, for-profit companies may continue to play a role by providing professional develop-ment opportunities and competing with one another for business, but teachers will not be compelled to receive training in any given area, especially when such an area is inextricably linked to the financial interest of a corporate entity (such as Common Core State Standards [CCSS] and its respective state assessment).

Third, as leaders, teachers must play an active role in how they will be evaluated and held to a standard of accountability. By no means should teach-ers be free from meaningful evaluation, nor should students. However, such evaluation must be multifaceted, fair, valid, and based on the expertise of other educationists and teachers. Further, such evaluations should not result in profiteering for private companies. Therefore, part of the teachers' role on the interdisciplinary council is to determine what those meaningful evalua-tions will be, with such evaluations being free to differ between content areas, grades, schools, or any other division deemed necessary by those teachers.

Leave Decisions for Teacher Preparation and Education to Educationists

A clear by-product of a culture of mistrust against teachers is the swift corpo-ratization of the teacher qualification realm, with the clearest example being the deep influence and financial interests of Pearson, Inc. in the permeation and commercialization of the Teacher Performance Assessment (edTPA), as well as a vast number of teacher certification tests. It is through this type of effort that the mistrust and devaluation of teachers is clearly extended to that of intellectual and academic educationists such as teacher educators, deans of schools of education, professors in related fields, among other stakeholders whose roles lie primarily in the realm of higher education.

Just as external, corporate agencies have infiltrated the decision-making process on public education, so, too, have they infiltrated the decision-making processes in teacher certification. This has not led, in any way, to increased teacher quality, as there are currently no studies validating the effectiveness of edTPA or more rigorous testing requirements for pre-certified teachers on teacher effectiveness or student achievement. It has led, however, to a vast increase in profiteering by publishing and educational testing companies, and a tacit but systematic exclusion of financially unprivileged preservice teachers who are now required to pay several thousands of dollars to engage in these ultimately meaningless exercises that have little, if any, actual bearing on their teaching practice and effectiveness.

While there is, indeed, a sizable faction of teacher educators who believe in the validity of edTPA, some of whom are directly affiliated with its corporate interest and some of whom are not, there is an equally sizable faction, if not a majority, of educationists do not support it in either concept or practice based on both intellectual as well as humanitarian grounds. It is essential, then, for the decision latitude regarding entrance requirements, coursework requirements, field experience requirements, evaluation requirements, and any other relevant requirements to be deemed certified to be relegated to teacher educators and teacher education programs.

Individual programs must be given the latitude to address teacher preparation from their own vantages, philosophies, and methodological perspectives, so long as those perspectives can be validated by meaningful and valid forms of research. Further, it must be permissible for schools of education (or programs of teacher preparation) to differ from one another in both philosophy and curricular implementation and still be qualified to certify teachers according to their own guidelines. Teachers should not represent a monolithic faction with identical beliefs, methodologies, and sentiments regarding instruction. Rather, the very philosophical and methodological plurality that multiple teachers contribute should be the epicenter of American education.

EQUALIZING RELATIONSHIPS BETWEEN TEACHERS AND ADMINISTRATORS

Finally, the hierarchical and inequitable relationships between teachers and administrators must be vastly reformed. While supervisory systems are undoubtedly necessary in any organization and should be maintained to some degree, a totally egalitarian practice for truly administrative matters is not proposed. However, matters involving direct instructional services must be relegated directly to the teachers.

Administrative practices including mandatory curricula, limited or eliminated choice in textbook use, materials, scheduling, and instructional styles, and prescribed language (see the New York State Modules[9]) is directly adverse to a system of trust. Instead, all decisions made must be the product of respectful and trustful discourse between teachers and administrators in the context of the interdisciplinary council, with administrators serving an advisory role in areas of instruction, and teachers serving as an advisory role in areas of administration. Areas that affect both equally (or nearly equally) must be dealt with in a truly collaborative process through the council.

Similarly to teachers, administrators must be held to a form of evaluation that can also be determined by other administrators, with teachers playing an advisory role. If it is to be held that schools are to play an active role in the amelioration of social ills and there is to be genuine, valid, and meaningful accountability, it stands to reason that administrators at all levels (not just building levels) be held to meaningful scrutiny as well. Similarly to teachers, these evaluations should be multifaceted and informed by a number of factors.

ELIMINATE TEACHER UNION VILIFICATION

The tension between teacher unions and both the general public as well as political factions have long been a problematic area for all aspects of educational functioning. While the media often contribute to the image of teacher unions as militant, unrealistic, and representative of a special interest group for themselves (as opposed to their students), these characterizations are often aggrandized and caricaturized in a way that serves media-based sensationalism and political diversion more than anything else. As a result of many neoliberal and broad-stroked government initiatives, unions have been forced into a reactive position. According to a recent study,

> large scale federal policies such as No Child Left Behind and Race to the Top have undermined the strength of collective bargaining. The intensity of recent condemnations has caused teacher unions to take a number of different approaches: reacting defensively, accommodating to reform initiatives proposed by others, developing partnerships with education officials, and forging new reform directions on their own.[10]

It is the latter efforts, however, that represent more thoroughly what the unions ought to do, and have, in many cases, been trying to do. Undoubtedly unions are imperfect organizations, and are as prone to poor leadership, accountability, political corruption at various levels, and self-interest in certain respects as any other. Indeed, it would be inaccurate and imprudent to claim that all teacher unions are pure and without poor direction; neither would it be reasonable to claim that they are not politically connected and, in certain areas, politically motivated.

However, teacher unions are, in large part, service-based organizations that advocate for favorable working conditions in order to maximize the school environment for students. In light of the high level of mistrust that undoubtedly exists between many administrators and teachers, unions are, in many cases, the only tool by which teachers can advocate and progress toward organizational injustice, which is a clearly documented challenge in public schools.

FAIR WARNING

Lest these ideas appear to be radically apologetic of teachers, earnest attention must also be paid to the clear and present dangers of the narrow and protective views that can, and indeed have, come of certain union-led initiatives as well as an apathy and obdurateness that would be foolish and hypocritical to ignore. That is, if teachers are going to continue to advocate for fair, equitable, and meaningful forms of evaluation for themselves as well as their students, there must also be a willingness to accept change within the job description and historically typical duties of the teacher.

That is, some approaches to assessment, while clearly more fair and representative of the true nature of teaching may, in fact, require more time commitment. For example, the use of portfolios to assess student growth will require the creation of one portfolio per child that is regularly updated, maintained, and analyzed. This will, most assuredly, require far more time and effort, at least at the outset of design, than would standardized tests; incorporating such a mode of accountability, though more fair, would essentially also be requiring more quantitative and qualitative demand of teachers.

While it is reasonable for teachers to expect a respective change in time and/or compensation opportunities to allow for this change, these terms need to be ubiquitously fair, with some of the time and effort spent to be seen as an investment on the teacher's end in a system that they, themselves, helped to design, and an expansion of the teacher's typical role.

Essentially, a true effort toward educational reform with primary teacher decision latitude must not be distilled into an argument over expectations, job descriptions, contract stipulations, and compensation. Adjustments to these aspects must be made to represent a vast difference and increase in effort and job responsibility. However, these adjustments must also represent the time and effort that teachers will also *give* in order to be a constructive part of a changing educational landscape.

By making school practices in the area of instructional and accountability not necessarily more equitable in that all have equal latitude, but more equitable in that those that have the most level of expertise in the given area have more latitude, a culture of trust and respect, as well as expertise, is cultivated more directly. This minimizes the opportunities for external influence that is misguided, and allows for a truly constructive environment to foster what schools are meant to do: provide a facility for teaching and learning.

NOTES

1. Wayne K. Hoy & C. John Tarter. "Organizational Justice in Schools: No Justice without Trust." *International Journal of Educational Management*, 18 no. 4, (2004), 250–259.

2. Ibid.

3. Wayne K. Hoy. "Faculty Trust: A Key to Student Achievement." *Journal of School Public Relations*, 32 no. 2, (2002), 88–103.

4. Karen Seashore Louis. "Trust and Improvement in Schools." *Journal of Educational Change*, 8 no. 1, (2007), 1–24.

5. Karen Seashore Louis. "Changing the Culture of Schools: Professional Community, Organizational Learning, and Trust." *Journal of School Leadership*, 16, (2006), 477–489.

6. Anthony S. Bryk and Barbara Schneider. "Trust in Schools: A Core Resource for School Reform." *Educational Leadership*, 60 no. 6, (2003), 40–45.

7. Marja-Kristiina Lerkkanen, Eve Kikas, Eija Pakarinen, Pirjo-Liisa Poikonen, and Jari-Erik Nurmi. "Mothers' Trust toward Teachers in Relation to Teaching Practices," *Early Childhood Research Quarterly*, 28, (2013), 153–165.

8. http://www.highered.nysed.gov/tcert/.

9. https://www.engageny.org/resource/curriculum-module-update-list.

10. Nina Bascia and Pamela Osmond. (2012). "Teacher Unions and Educational Reform: A Research Review." National Education Association Center for Great Public Schools Research Department. Retrieved from https://feaweb.org/_data/files/ED_Reform/Teacher_Unions_and_Educational_Reform.pdf.

Chapter 11

Citizenship

A Local and Global Necessity for a True Value to Schooling

The importance of participation in local and larger scale governance has clearly been demonstrated to be a fundamental concept of true democratic functioning. However, it is not merely the participation in governance that matters most; rather, it is the cultivation of one's citizenship at both a local and global level that will allow the individual to understand why, and not just how, participation empowers democracy.

When one becomes a true citizen of his or her locale as well as his or her nation and world, one will begin to see the depth with which all cultures, and people within those cultures, are interdependent and inter-reliant in a swiftly globalizing society. The key to true cultivation of citizenship is not only acceptance, but the valuation of cultural pluralism, especially the deep belief in the idea that though cultures may perceive many or even all aspects of their reality differently, all perceptions and interpretations are legitimate and can be used to deepen and strengthen bonds both within and between ways of being.

Citizenship can be regarded in a number of different ways. Some conceptualizations, especially those steeped in a liberal tradition rely more heavily on the "being" of a citizen from which rights and responsibilities are bestowed upon an individual by a state (or nation). That is, one is *born* a citizen and remains one, regardless of whether those rights and responsibilities are fulfilled or at all utilized.

More progressive notions of citizenship, however, place the importance of citizenship on the "action" of a citizen, in which one is only truly a citizen if he or she actively participates in the making and shaping of his or her society, rather than simply one who "uses and chooses" its most preferable or personally beneficial aspects.[1] From this perspective, participation is seen as both a right and an obligation, not merely an invitation. Essentially, the right of participation in decision-making in social, economic, cultural and political life should be included in the nexus of basic human rights. . . . Citizenship as participation can be seen as representing an expression of human agency in the political arena, broadly defined; citizenship as rights enables people to act as agents.[2]

But in a time where globalization is unmistakably becoming a more significant qualifier of our citizenship duties, it is necessary to begin to explore and extend the notion of citizenship to encompass local, national, and global contexts as citizens' obligations also increasingly extend to these far-reaching areas. This concept, however, comes part and parcel with a number of controversies, with a significant one being how one is to balance (or replace) their obligations to their local and national ties (indeed, the state and country which certifies its membership and citizenship to begin with) with their global ties, a far less formalized and structured membership though one with great significance. As Myers suggests:

> Discussing the role of education in developing citizenship puts schools in the midst of conflict over social and institutional values. To propose that the educational system should develop global as well as national citizens is controversial. . . . Schools are alternately accused of undermining patriotism when they allow critical discussion of government policy and of narrow ethnocentrism when they neglect the critical examination of global issues.[3]

Inherent in the concept of global citizenship, then, is a clear rejection of assimilationist frameworks both in curriculum design as well as curricular practice. As demonstrated, this represents a major systemic shift in the very foundation of American education as, from its very roots in even post-Revolutionary America, one of the foundational purposes of schooling was to establish that very "American identity." This American identity may not, by design, be assimilationist, but clearly has become that way in the dominant educational and overall cultural narrative and social practices.

The assimilationist perspective clearly contends that the rights of groups are to be seen as antagonistic to the rights of the individual and, therefore, individuals must forfeit their ties to their groups, including language, cultural traditions, and cultural loyalty to their newfound individualism, which is, in itself, a hallmark of American culture.[4] Put more clearly:

> In the liberal assimilationist view, the rights of the individual are paramount, and group identities and rights are inconsistent with and inimical to the rights of the individual. This conception maintains that identity groups promote group rights over the rights of the individual and that the individual must be freed of

primordial and ethnic attachments to have free choice and options in a modernized democratic society. Strong attachments to ethnic, racial, religious, and other identity groups lead to conflicts and harmful divisions within society.[5]

Examples of this dominant modality of thinking and its reinforcement in the school system are multitudinous and applicable across a number of groupings throughout history including those based on race, ethnicity, language, gender, religion, and "ability" among others.

The major fallacy in this perspective, however, is the assumption that the problem of social justice violations lies within one's loyalty to their group, not the clearly demonstrated systematic marginalization of the groups themselves by the hegemonic practice. From this perspective, the very "ties" that liberal assimilationist perspectives denounce for the sake of "individual rights" can be easily viewed as a means of disenfranchisement as well. That is, it is far easier for an individual to get lost in a society that has disparate access to resources without backlash than it is for an entire community, as an individual has no group that he or she can grasp, while groups gain and retain power in numbers. This is a far more facilitative means of maintaining dominance than to have to manage a number of groups who consistently and effectively unite for the purpose of opposing and reversing oppressive practices.

In order to nurture the achievement of global citizenship, then, the very nature of citizenship itself must change fundamentally. It must develop to both consume and extend one's locality and nation to incorporate all of global civilization without the permissiveness of a dominant group (even such a group that straddles international and "cultural" boundaries in the name of power and dominance) to form. As Ladson-Billings suggests:

> The dynamic of modern (or postmodern) nation-state makes identities as either an individual or a member of a group untenable. Rather than seeing the choice as either/or, the citizen of the nation-state operates in the realism of both/and. She is both an individual who is entitled to citizen rights that permit one to legally challenge infringement of those rights. . . . People move back and forth across many identities and the way society responds to these identities either binds people to or alienates them from the civic culture.[6]

ELEMENTS OF A CURRICULUM THAT FACILITATES GLOBAL CITIZENSHIP

It is within a nonassimilationist framework that both the social focus and the curriculum delivery within schools need to be earnestly reevaluated in terms of its very purpose and function in a globalizing society. When conceptualizing how such a practice is to be facilitated, it is important that two overarching questions remain ever in focus: (1) What is the role of pluralism in the new curriculum? and (2) What is the role of competition in the new curriculum?

These questions are essential and interconnected in that both deal directly with the notion of dominance, the very foundation upon which assimilationist perspectives and curricula are built. That is, if dominance of one group (or one ideology) is to be maintained, an assimilationist framework must be preserved under any circumstances, as the dominant ideology will both blatantly and tacitly shape the way in which the curriculum is delivered, discussed, and engaged with.

Promoting a Culture of True Balance and Value in Pluralism

The most formidable opponent to the establishment of dominance, especially in a culture that already has strong and deep hegemonic roots among the white upper and middle class is to systematically, but radically, incorporate counter-narratives into the curriculum in a real and valued way. That is, patronizing efforts to incorporate pluralism in curriculum such as "Black History Month" and various periodic "awareness" projects are not genuine efforts to change the dominant narrative, but rather proverbial "bones" that are "thrown" to marginalized groups as a means of ceremonious, disingenuous recognition. These superficial efforts are not likely to produce any substantive social change. Such notions are entrenched in the global citizenship discourse.

Put forth originally by Fisher and Hicks as *world studies* or "studies which promote the knowledge, attitudes, and skills that are relevant to living responsibly in a multicultural and interdependent world," the central concepts include: (a) the study of cultures and countries that are different from one's own, especially by explicitly acknowledging and exploring such differences and similarities; (b) the study of major issues which face different countries, especially those including peace and conflict, inequality, development, human rights, and the environment; and (c) deeply exploring ways in which one's everyday life is affected (and affects) the wider world.[7]

Using these three bases, teachers must ensure that student engagement focuses on learning morally and socially responsible behavior, being involved in one's community, and attaining the knowledge, skills, and values for serving an effective role in public life, known also as political literacy.[8] Teachers must also take care to immerse students in the actions of global citizenship, deliberately suffusing its elements across the classroom environment and into the very school culture.

Sheldon Berman suggests that communities intent on cultivating a culture of global citizenship must create: (a) a nurturing and caring environment in which children are involved in decision making and prosocial action both in the home and at school; (b) adult modeling of specific prosocial and ethical behavior; (c) development of perspective-taking skills that provide young people the opportunity to enter (if only conceptually) the world of another individual and identify with their experience (such as injustice or inequality); and (d) allowing for explicit confrontations with injustice and exploring productive and constructive ways in which they can be handled and resolved.[9] Ultimately, this calls for a heavy emphasis on "transformative citizenship," or promoting civil actions that are designed to actualize the values, principles, and ideals that exist beyond current laws and social conventions, especially those that are unjust.[10]

What needs careful attention and central functioning, however, is true pluralism: that is, that *all* worldviews, whether they are controversial or commonplace, orthodox or moderate, radical or mainstream that are represented in a community be given voice to one degree or another. How much voice, in what context such voice is afforded space, and to what degree such perspectives will be discussed, endorsed, refuted, or otherwise dealt with must be left up to the interdisciplinary councils created by the local districts themselves.

However, it is fundamental that all stakeholders in the community and, especially in the school, be afforded the opportunity to have their views be given a place somewhere in the curriculum. As such, no topics, events, interpretations of events, or stories concerning the histories, journeys, and experiences of particular people can be seen as taboo. Indeed, if such perspectives may appear hateful, discriminatory, offensive, or violating in any way (such as overt racism and anti-Semitism a la neo-Nazi viewpoints, Ku Klux Klan, and certain factions of the Nation of Islam) these subjects may be elected to be handled in a special format (for instance, by reading a passage and facilitating a discussion without a direct representative of the thinking).

However, as a pivotal aspect of global citizenship is the context of human rights, it is equally as important to be aware of those agencies and ideologies that are likely to cause such violations as it is to know agencies that work against it.

Promoting a Culture of True Civic Participation Centered on Human Rights

The most formidable challenge for any curriculum based on global citizenship is that of human rights. The violation of human rights, by at least some citizens upon others, is a staple of any society regardless of how effortful means of suppressing such actions are in a culture. While there are, indeed, parties that would prefer, if not insist, that such violations are kept secret or, if revealed, not dealt with in public discourse, the continuity of human rights violations of any kind is the true antithesis of democracy.

Violations of human rights are, indeed, a complex issue, and one that is tied to virtually every aspect of democratic discussion. It is ultimately up to the students themselves to identify and address the multitude of ways in which human rights can be violated, but first effort must be paid to what human rights violations actually are in and of themselves.

Curricular efforts to actualize human rights as an issue must include close study and scrutiny of local, national, and international documents that address definitions, conceptualizations, violations, and consequences for such violations of human rights. Further, the ways in which such conceptualizations of human rights interact with the local, national, and global rights of others (specifically, those whose rights are *not* being violated) should be analyzed as a demonstration of true effects of global issues on personal lives and local happenings.[11]

Indicative in this study is also a means by which students can reconcile the differences between "local" and "global," especially in the context of interaction. As Myers suggests:

> Rather than a strictly universal teleology, with which the term "global" is often associated . . . the concept of global citizenship is concerned—not with processes of uniformity and homogeneity—but firstly with the intersections and dependencies of the local with the global (sometimes called "glocalization").[12]

Myers is careful to note, however, that this concept is not intended to suggest that local and national issues are to be ignored or simply absorbed into greater global ones. Rather, they should be seen in terms of their interdependency.

The purpose of such projects, however, must be clearly fixed on the aspect of civic participation and advocacy. The traditional means of governance, especially those of "party politics," has been shown to be of distinct disinterest to youth.[13] As a result, the importance of political participation is minimized, thus allowing the hegemonic state to be maintained and become increasingly unrepresentative of the greater population.

Evidence does indicate that youth are likely to become involved with social movements, especially those that have a direct relation to their everyday lives. This suggests that it is not the participation itself that is problematic, but rather the means by which participation is required in a traditional governmental structure. By reconceptualizing civic participation for youth in terms of participatory democracy, and demonstrating how such participation can actually change policy, practice, and ultimately culture, youth can be revitalized to become social and civic actors, disrupting, if not dismantling, the current nonrepresentative hegemonic system. Further, according to Myers, such an orientation . . . would not consist of dogmatically expecting students to take up certain causes but would explore emerging aspects of global politics: diverse forms of action, new agencies and organizations, targets of political activism, and reasons for political participation. It would consist of knowledge of the concepts and practices of global governance, global democracy, and global civil society, and their challenges. . . . A key focus would be to highlight the ways that local and national political issues are connected to global political issues.[14]

Promoting a Culture of Global Citizenship and Participation over Global Competitiveness

Finally, the notion of global competitiveness that has become so endemic to discussions of education must be replaced indelibly with that of global citizenship, participation, and collaboration. It must be explicitly noted, however, that focusing on global citizenship does not mean that discussions of economic contribution, significant roles of particular countries or cultures in specified areas, and the legitimate right to believe in one's culture and its importance must be eliminated. Quite the contrary, such discussions are an integral part of global citizenship. The deleterious component, however, is that of dominance, if not conquest. This poses a particular paradox to the context of globalization in the United States. According to Myers:

Much of the world considers globalization as synonymous for "Americanization" and an instrument of US hegemony. Many fear that globalization is overwhelming local cultures through the spread of homogenous popular culture. At the same time, within the US there are conservative fears that cultural pluralism is causing [Americans] to lose their national identity and the "American way of life."[15]

Such a conceptualization forces citizenship to function almost entirely superficially in the "legal citizenship" realm, which applies to citizens who are legal members of the nation-state and possess particular rights and responsibilities, but do not utilize them in any meaningful participatory way. As such, the status quo is maintained and the power elite are able to maintain their own agenda of colonization in the name of globalization. Such rhetoric is nearly ubiquitous in governmental stations. The website for the White House exclaims "to create true middle class security, we must out-innovate, out-educate, and out-build the rest of the world."[16]

Global competitiveness is further connected to education, as demonstrated in Obama's 2011 State of the Union address, in which he said:

Nations like China and India realized with some changes of their own, they could compete in the new world, and so they started educating their children earlier and longer, with greater emphasis on math and science.

By engaging in such rhetoric the notion of the "other" is starkly maintained, and perpetuates the idea that there must be a "winner." But what is seldom, if ever discussed, is what such a "winner" wins, and at whose expense. And further, what about the "loser?" Therefore, it is clear that maintaining the notion of competitiveness will propagate a process based both in secrecy and poaching. Secrecy, to the extent that nations will be less willing, if not overtly opposed to engaging in dialogue about new ideas, technologies, means of living that can potentially create a better global culture; poaching to the extent that, as a result of the secrecy, countries will be forced to compel the leaders of such new ideas to leave their place of origin and contribute to another country that has more to offer, so long as their contribution matches the reward.

While the marketization perspective has ever, and will likely continue to hold competition as its hallmark, there is little argument, especially from outside of the financially secure wealthy minority that uninhibited, capitalistic competition has been far more harmful than beneficial, and has, without doubt, exceedingly exacerbated the inequity of power and stratification of wealth on a global level.

Conversely, global citizenship minimizes the occurrence of secrecy and thus eliminates the need for poaching. Rather, focusing on global citizenship allows individuals across cultures to both recognize and capitalize on their interdependence, creating an opportunity for collaboration and, potentially, synergistic innovation that can be universally beneficial. With such a focus the workings of a democratic global community would become far more self-sufficient and the need for "over-governance" far less necessary. Indeed, it is idealistic to presume that the elimination of greed, especially by those who have amassed so much under the current system. However, it is far less idealistic to assume that, by empowering the vast majority, the vast minority must, in turn, lose some of its undeserved influence and the "scales" will begin to "tip" the opposite way.

NOTES

1. Gaventa, "Towards a Participatory Governance."
2. Ruth Lister. "Citizen in Action: Citizenship and Community Development in Northern Ireland Context." *Community Development Journal*, 33 no. 3, (1998), 226–235.
3. J. P. Myers. "Rethinking the Social Studies Curriculum in the Context of Globalization: Education for Global Citizenship in the U.S." *Theory and Research in Social Education*, 34 no. 3, (2006), 370–394.
4. James A. Banks. "Diversity, Group Identity, and Citizenship Education in a Global Age." *Educational Researcher*, 37 no. 3, (2008), 129–139.

5. Ibid.
6. Gloria Ladson-Billings. "Culture versus Citizenship: The Challenge of Racialized Citizenship in the United States." In J. A. Banks (Ed.) *Diversity and Citizenship in Education: Global Perspectives* (pp. 99–126) (San Fransisco: Jossey-Bass, 2004).
7. Simon Fisher and David Hicks. *World Studies 8–13: A Teacher's Handbook.* (Edinburgh, UK: Oliver & Boyd, 1985).
8. Cathie Holden (2000). "Learning for Democracy: From World Studies to Global Citizenship." *Theory into Practice*, 39 no. 2, (2000), 74–80.
9. Sheldon Berman. *Children's Social Consciousness and the Development of Social Responsibility.* (Albany, NY: SUNY Press, 1997).
10. Banks, "Diversity."
11. Myers, "Rethinking the Social Studies Curriculum."
12. Ibid.
13. Ibid.
14. Ibid.
15. Ibid.
16. https://www.whitehouse.gov/economy/business/competing-globally.

Chapter 12

A Place for Everyone

Culturally Responsive Teaching

Global citizenship relies not only on acceptance and tolerance, but also on deep and genuine valuation of multiple cultures both within and outside of America. While American education has, indeed, made some progress in the area of incorporating elements of multiple cultures in its curriculum, in some ways an echo of national social changes such as Black History Month, Women's History Month, Martin Luther King Day, and other similar developments, these gestures remain largely ceremonious, suggesting merely symbolic valuation without actually committing to true incorporation into the dominant cultural narrative. In many ways these efforts may even represent a symbol of "starting over," that is a decisive exclamation that our country has moved beyond such discrimination and is now the embodiment of liberty.

A clear trend in America is the continual influx of immigrants from a variety of countries and cultures. Indeed, despite the challenges America faces socially and economically, the notion is that the "American Dream" is alive and well and continues to lure many to its soil. This influx has not been without its challenges, however, creating a number of issues for the immigrants themselves, as well as those who have already put down roots in America, be they nationally born or also an immigrant with longer residency. Among these challenges that are pertinent to the educational process is the increase in both culturally and linguistically diverse students in many classrooms, though much more largely represented in urban areas. As Brown suggests:

> The demographic shift in the United States is more apparent in the public schools than anywhere else. But this change in the racial, cultural, and linguistic diversity of the student population is not the problem. The problem lies in the way educators have responded to that change. A positive or negative response could affect the self-esteem and academic success of students from these varied

racial, cultural, and linguistic backgrounds. Therefore, many researchers have challenged schools and educators to find creative ways to work with students from culturally and linguistically diverse backgrounds.[1]

To meet this challenge of culturally and linguistically diverse students saturating American classrooms in a productive and constructive manner, a number of scholars have sought to widen and deepen the extent of multicultural education strategies, evolving what has instead become known as "culturally responsive teaching." While multiple definitions abound, a comprehensive means of conceptualizing culturally responsive educational systems are those that are

> grounded in the beliefs that all culturally and linguistically diverse students can excel in academic endeavors when their culture, language, heritage, and experiences are valued and used to facilitate their learning and development, and they are provided access to high quality teachers, programs, and resources.[2]

Essentially, culturally responsive teachers maintain the belief that the influence of culture is deeply entwined in the manner of student of learning, and that these cultural influences should be nurtured and capitalized on, rather than be replaced or dismissed. Not only must teachers reflect an appreciation and value for students' native culture, but use the essential aspects of that culture to create an inclusive, effective, and constructive classroom environment that is rich with value and learning. In order to do this, culturally responsive teachers must create classroom communities that

> specifically acknowledge the presence of culturally diverse students and the need for these students to find connections among themselves and with the subject matter and the tasks the teacher asks them to perform.[3]

The key basis of culturally responsive teaching is, indeed, a sensitive and controversial one. At its core, culturally responsive teachers must accept the notion that there is a deep and wide disproportionality between those individuals and values that are most notably valued in American society, particularly those of the white middle and upper-middle class, and those that are deeply devalued, particularly those of poor minority cultures.

To be clear, this is not to say that all valuation in society can be traced along racial and ethnic lines, as there is undoubtedly a presence of multiple cultures in the middle and upper-middle class. However, the presence of these individuals and families, however few, must be regarded as the exceptions that prove the rule, cementing the idea that one is valued in society only when the middle-class standard is attained. Thus, there is a complex interaction between racist and classist practices, resulting, in large part, in what many scholars refer to as "whiteness."

The idea of "whiteness" is a precarious and controversial one, as it is easily misrepresented as well as misunderstood.[4] As Leonardo suggests, "Whiteness is a racial discourse, whereas the category 'white people' represents a socially constructed identity, usually based on skin color."[5] More specifically,

> critical scholarship on whiteness is not an assault on white people per se; it is an assault on the socially constructed and constantly reinforced power of white identifications and interests.[6]

In this sense, whiteness is based more largely on action and cultural mechanism than it is on a passive role of skin color. According to Giroux,

> the critical project that largely informs the new scholarship on "whiteness" rests on a singular assumption. Its primary aim is to unveil the rhetorical, political, cultural, and social mechanisms through which "whiteness" is both invented and used to mask its power and privilege.[7]

In this sense, then, the role that "whiteness" plays lies far beyond blatant racist actions and acts of racial hatred. Rather, it lies more squarely in the power dynamic that has become so engrained in institutional, cultural, and social practice that it appears to be virtually inherent, and often goes either unnoticed or disputed in the context of the same superficial aforementioned ceremonies such as Black History Month and Martin Luther King Day. Indeed, the notion of race and "whiteness" as a critical component even in educational research and discourse, especially among white educational researchers, remains largely superficial with only a few notable exceptions in contributors like Giroux, Kincheloe, and McLaren.[8]

As Ansley suggests:

> White supremacy . . . [does not] . . . allude to the self-conscious racism of white supremacist hate groups. I refer, instead, to a political, economic, and cultural system in which whites overwhelmingly control power and material resources, conscious and unconscious ideas of white superiority and entitlement are widespread, and relations of white dominance and non-white subordination are daily reenacted across a broad array of institutions and social settings.[9]

Additionally, the notion of "whiteness" allows many white people to live in an illusory nonracial (or, in current terms, "post-racial") state. While propitious for white people themselves, this state is exponentially harmful for the state of social justice of the greater culture, creating high levels of insensitivity, intolerance and, in certain cases, blatant propagation of racist practices. A key result of this insular perspective is a lack of objectivity based on the function of race, resulting in the paradoxical and erroneous explanation that "white people" do not perceive social ideas in terms of race as other races do, while in fact their "whiteness" is equally as significant a factor as others' "non-whiteness."[10]

The role that "whiteness" plays in schooling is deeply complex, and in no way limited to those who are white in terms of their skin color. Rather, "whiteness" permeates all levels of culture as both a tacit and blatant standard toward which Americans, or anyone who resides in America, are to strive. In order to change the cultural context for "whiteness" as it plays out in schools, there are a number of realizations that teachers must make.

First, teachers must be willing to recognize that all people are cultural beings, and all possess their own beliefs, assumptions, and biases about human behavior. Second, teachers must acknowledge the reality that there are cultural, racial, ethnic, and class differences among people. Third, teachers must acknowledge the idea that schools both reflect and perpetuate discriminatory practices of those who do not meet the standard of "whiteness," and commit to working against these processes that are deeply engrained in school culture and practice.[11]

Weinstein and colleagues explain it this way:

> When teachers and students come from different cultural backgrounds, planned efforts to cross social borders and develop caring, respectful relationships are essential. From the very first day of school, teachers can set the tone by greeting students at the door with a smile and a warm, welcoming comment. Greeting second language learners with a phrase in their native language can be especially affirming. Teachers can also forge positive relationships with students by sharing stories about their lives outside of school, learning about students' interests and activities, inviting them to make choices and decisions about class activities, and listening to their concerns and opinions. It is critical that teachers deliberately model respect for diversity—by expressing admiration for a student's bilingual ability, by commenting enthusiastically about the number of different languages that are represented in class, and by including examples and content from a variety of cultures in their teaching.[12]

In this Weinstein makes it clear that students must know from the very beginning that they are not seen as outsiders, visitors, or immigrants expected to assimilate quickly and readily. Rather, they are entering an environment that deeply acknowledges, respects, and values their native culture, and actively looks for ways to incorporate them into the learning process. As Weinstein further admonishes:

Being a culturally responsive classroom [teacher] means more than learning a few words in a student's native language or creating bulletin board that highlights students' countries of origin. It means being willing to reflect on ways that classroom management decisions promote or obstruct students' access to learning. Culturally responsive classroom management is a *frame of mind* as much as a set of strategies or practices.[13]

Despite the importance of teachers becoming culturally responsive, however, there is a deeper issue that any polemic involving educational change must consider. The ways in which teacher preparation programs that produce American teachers are designed must deeply reflect the notion of multicultural valuation in a deep and genuine way. Indeed, the same deep and pervasive cultural notions of the dominance of "whiteness," often cloaked in a variety of other terms including "professionalism," "socially appropriate," "presentable," and others are largely preserved in teacher education programs.

While most state and national accreditation agencies now require that teacher preparation programs incorporate elements of multiculturalism in their program, such curricular changes have often reflected largely superficial, if not entirely ceremonious curricular adjustments such as adding a course in multiculturalism, absorbing the multicultural content in existing courses, or requiring students to accrue field experience in a "culturally and linguistically diverse," a clear euphemism for a predominantly black and Hispanic neighborhood for part of their fieldwork requirements.[14]

Though there is a growing body of research that examines how teacher preparation programs can enhance the presence of multiculturalism and, ultimately, culturally responsive teaching methods in their program, most studies merely examine the structural makeup of such programs. Few, if any of the studies, provide any meaningful information as to how such additional course-based topics actually contribute to teachers' ability to teach in a culturally responsive manner.[15] Additionally, the research that is available is largely disproportionate, focusing predominantly on white females (who continue to make up the largest demographic of teachers in America).[16]

Indeed, the ineffectiveness of teacher preparation regarding culturally and linguistically diverse students is, and has been ever-present.[17] The problem can be expressed this way:

The teacher turnover rate in the urban schools is much higher than in the suburban schools. . . . The result is that urban schools, especially those in inner cities, are often staffed largely by newly hired or uncertified teachers. These teachers, who were trained to teach students from middle class families and who often come from middle class families themselves, now find themselves engulfed by minority students, immigrants, and other students from low income families—students whose values and experiences are very different from their own.[18]

Clearly the superficial inclusion of an academically oriented curriculum in the area of multiculturalism or cultural responsiveness is largely in vain, as the numbers continue to represent disproportionately larger turnover rates in urban schools as compared to suburban schools, as well as suburban schools with a large minority population.[19,20] Teacher preparation programs can, however, begin to restructure themselves to be more genuinely contributive to the need for culturally responsive teachers. One potential way is by implementing a six-strand structure suggested by Villegas and Lucas.[21]

First, teacher preparation programs must promote sociocultural consciousness, or an understanding that race, class, culture, and language have a deep influence on people's ways of thinking. Second, teachers must adopt an affirming attitude toward culturally and linguistically diverse students, which requires them to accept the truth that "whiteness" is highly prized in American society. Third, culturally responsive teachers are capable of effectively changing the dominant cultural message to equally value the contributions of all of their students' cultures. Fourth, adopting a constructivist view of learning which holds central the idea that realities are created by and can vary between individuals is essential. Fifth, teachers must learn how to deeply engage with students nonjudgmentally regarding their family, social, and cultural lives. Finally, teachers must learn how to use what they know about their students to engage their learning.

Clearly maintaining a middle-classist and "whiteness" valued curriculum is detrimental to both individual students and society as a whole, forcing students to cast off their deeply important, if not essential aspects of their culture in order to assimilate to an archaic conceptualization of the "American." Culturally responsive teaching is undoubtedly an integral part of the antidote to the highly standardized and classist approaches of that the corporatization of schools has implemented. Without culturally responsive teaching the children of America risk retaining a pride in ignorance and exceptionalism that has done little but harm the greater society for decades, and turn the school, a place that should be the site of citizenship development, into an institution of dominance and oppression.

NOTES

1. Monica R. Brown. "Educating All Students: Creating Culturally Responsive Teachers, Classrooms, and Schools." *Intervention in School and Clinic*, 43, (2007), 57.

2. Janette Klingner, Alfredo J. Artiles, Elizabeth Kozelski, Beth Harry, Shelley Zion, William Tate, Grace Zemora Duran, and David Riley. "Addressing the Disproportionate Representation of Special Education through Cultural Responsive Educational Systems." *Education Policy Analysis Archives*, 13 no. 38 (2005). From http://epaa.asu.edu/ojs/article/view/143.

3. Montgomery, 2001, as cited by Brown, 60.

4. David Gillborn. "Education Policy as an Act of White Supremacy: Whiteness, Critical Race Theory, and Education Reform." *Journal of Education Policy*, 20 no. 4, (2005), 485–505.

5. Leonardo, 2004, as cited by Gillborn, "Education Policy," 7.

6. Gillborn, "Education Policy," 7–8.

7. Giroux, 1997, as cited by Gillborn, "Education Policy," p. 8.

8. Ricky Lee Allen. (2004). "Whiteness and Critical Pedagogy." *Educational Philosophy and Theory,* 36 no. 2, (2004), 121–136.

9. Ansley, 1997, as cited by Gillborn, "Education Policy," 11.

10. Robin DiAngelo. "White Fragility." *International Journal of Critical Pedagogy*, 3 no. 3, (2011), 54–70.

11. Carol Weinstein, Mary Curran, and Saundra Tomlinson-Clarke. "Culturally Responsive Classroom Management." *Theory into Practice*, 2 no. 4, (2003), 269–276.

12. Weinstein et al., "Culturally Responsive Classroom Management," 274.

13. Weinstein et al., "Culturally Responsive Classroom Management," 275.

14. Ana Maria Villegas and Tamara Lucas. "Preparing Culturally Responsive Teachers: Rethinking the Curriculum." *Journal of Teacher Education*, 53 no. 1, (2002), 20–32.

15. Christine E. Sleeter. "Preparing Teachers for Culturally Diverse Schools: Research and the Overwhelming Presence of Whiteness." *Journal of Teacher Education*, 52 no. 2, (2001), 94–106.

16. C. Emily Feistritzer (2011). "Profiles of Teachers in the U.S. 2011. National Center for Education Information." Retrieved from http://www.edweek.org/media/pot2011final-blog.pdf.

17. Dave F. Brown (2004). "Urban Teachers' Professed Classroom Management Strategies: Reflections of Culturally Responsive Teaching." *Urban Education*, 39 no. 3, 266–289.

18. E.A. Crosby "Urban Schools Forced to Fail" *Phi Delta Kappan.* 81 no. 4, (1999), 298–303, p. 302.

19. Nicole S. Simon and Susan Moore Johnson (2013). "Teacher Turnover in High Poverty Schools: What We Know and Can Do." Retrieved from http://isites.harvard.edu/fs/docs/icb.topic1231814.files/Teacher%20Turnover%20in%20High-Poverty%20Schools.pdf.

20. John Papay (2013). "What's Driving Teachers away from High Poverty Schools. Center on Great Teachers & Leaders." Retrieved from http://isites.harvard.edu/fs/docs/icb.topic1231814.files/Teacher%20Turnover%20in%20High-Poverty%20Schools.pdf.

21. Villegas and Lucas, "Preparing Culturally Responsive Teachers."

Chapter 13

Real Partnerships, Real Choice

Uniting Students, Teachers, and Parents to Effect Genuine Community Investment

It is virtually inarguable that there is clear race-based and class-based stratification between residential communities in the United States and these differences affect virtually every aspect of that community from commerce to education to political representation, and everything in between. While a significant amount of rhetoric has surrounded the devaluated attention that these communities have received resulting in a number of disadvantages, most notably the educational achievement gap, little genuine systematic effort has been put forth to truly invest in and rebuild these forgotten and forsaken communities, especially in the area of public education.

Instead, private corporate enterprises have partnered with public educational agencies to design and provide strategically placed alternative schools available to the residents of these communities with little action, or likely interest, in investing in the rest of the community to which their students return after school hours. While this has been successfully touted as educational reform and earnest attention to a key civil rights issue cloaked in the concept of "school choice" in the popular media, both quantitative data and sociocultural analysis make it glaringly clear that not only are these efforts ineffective educationally, but the true thrust of the endeavors is profiteering as opposed to the amelioration of social illsn.

The notion of social capital provides a relevant framework within which a model of genuine, whole-community investment can begin to be proffered. While elusive to capture, as are many other sociocultural terms, social capital will be regarded as the material and nonmaterial resources that are accessible to individuals and families primarily through their social ties.[1] That is, the greater, more vast, and more well connected one is to their community at all levels, the greater their access and influence within that community.[2]

Essentially, more frequent and more significant ties equal more frequent and more significant influence in the community decision-making processes. When applied to socioeconomically disadvantaged and disenfranchised communities, especially when recognizing that these communities are indelibly tied to race and ethnicity, it becomes clear that there is a systematic form of marginalization at work, which renders entire communities nearly powerless to self-advocate, leaving them only to be acted upon by other, more powerful and more wealthy entities.

Further, notions of both "internal social capital" as well as "external social capital" prove essential in the function (or dysfunction) of particular communities. Internal social capital, or those ties which can be acted upon within a community and between actors in that community, have a direct effect on how cohesive and self-interested that community is. High levels of internal social capital are likely to produce close-knit and mutually concerned communities, with community members having the ability to act on their own behalf. External social capital, conversely, refers to the ties that are forged outside of the community itself. Securing external social capital enables communities to receive resources from those outside of the community itself for use within it.

The concept of social capital provides a very applicable framework to understanding both the success of and the accessibility to challenged socioeconomic areas by corporately and politically connected charter school enterprises. That is, communities that are challenged socioeconomically are very likely to have low levels of both types of social capital, deeming the community nearly powerless in both internal and external matters. This powerlessness leaves community members ripe to be "acted upon" by others with high levels of both capitals, as well as an abundance of financial means. The result of this enactment has led to the propagation of powerlessness among the challenged socioeconomic communities as well as an increased level of dependence on corporate intervention.

Essentially, this phenomenon distills into a form of local colonization. That is, an underprivileged community with desperate need for intervention and reinvestment is unlikely to refuse aid from any agent, especially those that come with lofty promises such as improved schooling, increased opportunity, and higher standards for an ostensibly deteriorating neighborhood. Further, even if the community itself were resistant to such intervention, the likelihood of gathering enough power and influence to resist it is unlikely, if not impossible. As such, these communities are relegated virtually to defenseless "receptors" at the mercy of both the corporate system and the public bureaucracy, the lines between which have been almost entirely eliminated.

The solution, then, to anti-local-colonization in this case is no different than in any other case: empowering the oppressed to retake control of their community and its affairs, and secure genuine investment for it. The means by which to achieve such empowerment is through genuine community partnerships in which community members themselves increase their genuine usable social capital, are entitled to maintain self-identified elements of cultural importance without consequences, and local leaders and general community members are provided with actual participatory latitude in decision making regarding where investments go, how such money is to be used, and what function the schools in their community will serve. Ultimately, these communities must be enabled to devise their own interdisciplinary councils and reap the economic and social benefits of the investments in their community directly.

Cultivating Real Community Partnerships through Service Learning

There is a rich and growing literature that positively identifies deep benefits of service learning, especially in the area of both reducing antisocial action and violence in communities, as well as increasing prosocial and constructive action.[3] Service learning can be seen as an approach which involves:

> Students and teachers receiving information, skills, resources, and assistance to meet genuine needs; community agencies helping to meet needs that could not otherwise be met by paid school staff; a widening of understanding about community issues; and a pooling of services and resources to meet community needs.[4]

Ultimately, service learning efforts are not superficial, lesson-based exercises to expose students to the plight of others; rather, if employed with fidelity, it is a deep, genuine, and service-based experience in which the efforts of the students directly benefit and serve a real need in the community. Thus, there is not only reciprocal understanding of the deep connection between the school and community itself, but there is also a reciprocal functional benefit that comes directly out of the relationship which mutually strengthens each.

The essential elements of effective service learning, then, can be suggested to be: (1) effective and open communication and dialogue between all parties; (2) shared decision-making latitude; (3) shared resources between all parties; (4) provision of genuine expertise and credibility of efforts by external experts; (5) sufficient allotment of time to develop and maintain relationships before meaningful change can occur; (6) dedication and physical presence to activities by all members of the partnership; (7) flexibility in efforts, project, changing needs, and changing decision frameworks; (8) a strong and shared orientation of change and belief for the youth involved; and (9) recognition of potentially differing priorities between partners.[5]

Enabling Genuine Parental Participation in School-Community Projects

While much rhetoric centers on parental choice in schooling, few of the discussions, especially those involving charter schools, focus on the direct role that parents play beyond simply choosing their desired school location for their children, a rather passive action and a mere social gesture overall. Likely, this is due to the fact that there are no other real opportunities for parents to be involved in, and parents who are a part of such socioeconomically challenged communities are likely to have fewer opportunities to be meaningfully involved based on additional obligations including work. The charter school effort, while emphasizing student achievement and educational opportunity, has simultaneously contributed to the increasing isolation between the communities themselves and their schools, especially in urban areas.[6]

Genuine partnerships between parents and schools depend on a number of systematic changes, but are also based on a number of perceptual adjustments that are deeply woven into the cultural conceptualization of challenged socioeconomic communities. The tendency for society at large to blame the community itself (if not the "degenerative" nature of the culture of those who inhabit these communities) has been historically demonstrated across at least two centuries in the United States, with examples dating even farther if pre-Revolutionary history is considered.

As a result, an adversarial relationship is often maintained between school officials and parents and students. These acrimonious relationships translate into reciprocal blaming for the deleterious state of schools in these communities, with officials often identifying cultural deprivation, dysfunctional family structure, and antisocial and degenerative community values as the source, while families and students are more apt to blame the systematic racism, discrimination, and insensitivity of school personnel.[7] Essentially, there are deep and consistent reciprocal violations of institutional trust.

Indeed, there are likely regrettable realities to both perspectives. However, the solution lies not in determining on whom the blame should be correctly laid, but rather how those elements that are misconceptions are resolved, and those elements that are, indeed, realities, are corrected.

The key to the success of such partnerships appears to lie in three main areas. The first is establishing an emphasis on relationship building both among and between parents and educators within the community and the school system. While this is essential for any effort to be successful, it is imperative, as was the case in service learning, that relationship be given enough time to develop.

The second is in focusing efforts on developing leadership skills among the parents themselves. Allowing parents to become leaders increases not only their social capital and decision latitude in the community, but also their sense of obligation to act on behalf of the whole community's well-being and health.

The third is bridging the gap in both culture and power between parents and educators. Indeed, since schooling is a shared enterprise with all stakeholders having involvement with the main beneficiary, the students, it must be recognized and respected that though all are acting on behalf of the children there may be different conceptualizations, methodologies, and priorities between stakeholders.[8]

Fulfillment of these priorities need not be based on dominance or control, but rather in shared decision making. Indeed, this is not to say that parents' and teachers' powers need to be equalized on all fronts (as mentioned in a previous chapter, teachers should be given more latitude in areas of instruction). However, power does not need to be equalized in order to be fair and just. Availability of information and decision-making latitude, even if not in terms of having the "final say" are both incredibly important means of inclusion for families who have, most likely, previously experienced total exclusion.

A prudent means by which this process can be started is by assembling a council in which resources are evaluated and inventoried. That is, the assumption that though a community has significant socioeconomic challenges there are likely no resources and no community-based organizations or structure must be eliminated. Indeed, though the community may be challenged, it is evident that there are elements, if not strong presences, of community-based organizations, whether formal or informal in many disenfranchised neighborhoods. These organizations must be capitalized on, legitimized, and empowered as leaders in the effort. Once the presence of such resources is identified, it is equally as important to determine the resources that are not available, and strategize as to how they are to be accessed in a way that is fair and not based on exploitation or profiteering.

Strong community partnerships have been shown to have a propitious effect on student performance as a whole, not only in the narrow conceptual area of academic achievement. School-community partnerships effectively facilitate the overlapping students' "spheres of influence," or realms from which an individual's behavior, lifestyle, choice-making tendencies, and overall culture are derived. As a result, there are clear connections between infusing positive and constructive influences into these realms and fostering a sense of community and connectivity, which leads to improved behavior, as well as a greater sense of obligation to one's locality.[9] Evidence of this greater sense of connection can be garnered through improvements in student attendance.[10]

One example of an effective, though imperfect, school-community partnership in Chicago, one of America's most segregated and challenged cities, is that of the Comprehensive Community Initiative (CCI), facilitated by the

Jones Family Foundation. Initially designed as a ten-year commitment with an annual budget of $350,000 or more, the initiative intended to use its resources to foster the development of Chicago's youth by enhancing community members' social capital (seen as trusting and supportive networks between schools and other community institutions), human capital (seen as the capacity of teachers , principals, and youth workers to enact influence), and financial capital (seen as funds available for developing both social and human capital).[11]

Essentially the effort was effective in most capacities, especially in its ability to initiate and maintain ties between all stakeholders. Further, principals, teachers, and students all indicated that a sense of trust and value between partners was facilitated as a result of the project. In contrast, however, early efforts lacked clear definition of roles as well as an insufficient alignment with specific school needs, resulting in overextension and initial disappointment in the effort. As a result, a true implementation of flexibility and shared decision making was needed to adjust and realign the needs with resources.

The Chicago CCI and other school-community initiatives demonstrate a clear lesson. While schools are, undoubtedly, one of the pillars of a propitious community, history has shown repeatedly that focusing all efforts on school reform without simultaneous efforts in the whole community and greater society itself will undoubtedly remain fruitless.[12] The lingering abject state of schools in challenged socioeconomic areas is a testament to this truth. If America is to truly experience the amelioration of social ills, fairness in accessibility, and true democratic functioning, the entirety of the community must receive the efforts of investment.

Facilitating Trust between Teachers and Students

While service learning efforts and community partnerships are essential to genuine investment in communities, neither is capable of effecting any change if the relationship between the students and their teachers is challenged. Though there are a number of means in which teacher-student relationships can be conceptualized, it appears that one of the most essential elements is trust (which is no different than the discussion involving the valuation of teachers). Indeed, without trust there is to be no sense of value, nor any sense of democracy as the participants will not be deemed worthy or able to exercise their right to participation.

Further, without trust in both the schools and its most important agents, the teachers, students will be unlikely to attend and therefore never get the opportunity to build a relationship with his or her community to begin with. Therefore, the most essential relationship to cultivate, before any other accomplishments can be realized, is between the student and the teacher.

Indeed, in urban schools a culture of suspicion and even criminality is often more dominant than that of trust and cooperation. As will be explored in the next chapter, zero tolerance efforts and criminalization of school-based behaviors have proven cantankerous to any semblance of a democratic culture in urban schools, especially those that are primarily attended by black and Hispanic students. While these efforts reflect the increasing emphasis on punitive methods in greater American society, there is virtually no evidence to demonstrate its effect on student behavior in any positive way, with studies actually indicating the contrary. Essentially, the sense of authority that is seen as central to the disciplinary success of schools has been shown to largely be a failure. Put this way:

> Schools attempt to convince students, though not always successfully, that the rules and controls to which they are subjected and the often tedious or onerous assignments that they are given represent the legitimate exercise of their authority rather than the arbitrary use of their power.[13]

In other words, teachers and school officials are seldom seen as legitimate authority figures, but rather as actors who exercise such authority without true purpose.

Conversely, a growing literature is beginning to support the importance of facilitating trust in students, rather than presuming suspicion or guilt. A number of these studies take on the perspective of Positive Behavior Support (PBS, known also by a number of other monikers such as School-Wide Positive Behavior Support, Positive Behavior Intervention, Positive Behavior Intervention and Support, among others).[14]

These models, when implemented in an "early response" context, can be vastly more effective than "zero tolerance" approaches.[15] This methodology capitalizes on behavior analytic learning theory, which generally posits that behavior is manipulated by the consequences in an environment and, with systematic implementation, intervention plans that focus on both reward and punishment and define behaviors in observable terms can be effective at modulating the behavior of students school-wide.

Other studies focus more readily on the idea of trust itself, focusing not only on the observable rules and provisions of external reward as in PBS, but also on cultivating the emotional and developmental bonds between teachers and students as an internal as well as external process. While in PBS the power source remains at the level of authority (i.e., when the behavioral contingency is fulfilled or violated an authority figure will provide the reward or punishment, respectively), methods capitalizing on relational trust seek to enact processes in which power is equalized or shared between student and teacher.

This can be achieved through a number of means. One such means is authorizing student perspectives, which recognizes and respects the profound ways in which the world has changed, and continues to change, and ultimately affects the position of the student in school and extracurricular life. Better explained:

Authorizing student perspectives introduces into critical conversations the missing perspectives of those who experience daily the effects of existing educational policies-in-practice. . . . By virtue of their saturation in information technology, youth cultural media, and political currents like those set in motion by globalization, students are differently knowledgeable about the range of new modes of communication and uses for education than the teachers and educational researchers who work with them. Given their experience and perspectives, and given their position in a rapidly changing world, students must assume a different role in education and reform than they have, up until recently, been afforded.[16]

Other research efforts are beginning to indicate the strong correlation between teachers' perceptions of their students' abilities and academic performance and behavior. Indeed, while these perceptions often remain tacit, it is becoming clear that they are acted upon in the context of teacher-student interactions. Furthermore, it is becoming ever clearer that students can infer teachers' perceptions of them.

This aspect of the teacher-student relationship is closely related to the level of trust felt between them. That is, a student who perceives low expectations from the teachers is not likely to develop trust as compared to those who perceive high expectation. As such, facilitating teachers' trust in all of their students, in many cases regardless of their preconceived notions or biases, is essential.[17]

It is clear that without full investment in the entire community, including the students themselves, parents, and other community stakeholders, educational reform will have no effect on social problems. Without full investment, the same underresourced, underappreciated, and politically marginalized community is left intact, making no difference in its ability to act upon itself in its own self-interest.

This maintenance of status quo provides for the propagation of local colonization as well as continued oppression. The only true source of effective educational reform is by earnestly and genuinely investing in the entire community in a way that fosters local leadership, cultural reverence, community-based decision making, and financial support for the true needs of the community.

NOTES

1. Erin McNamara Horvat, Elliot B. Weininger, and Annette Lareau. "From Social Ties to Social Capital: Class Differences in the Relations between Schools and Parent Networks." *American Educational Research Review*, 40 no. 2, (2003), 319–351.

2. Pedro Noguera (2004). "Social Capital and the Education of Immigrant Students" Sociology of Education, 77, no. 2, 180–183.

3. Linda M. Bosma, Renee E. Sieving, Annie Ericson, Pamela Russ, Laura Cavender, and Mark Bonne. "Elements for Successful Collaboration between K-12 School, Community Agency, and University Partners: The Lead Peace Partnership." *Journal of School Health*, 80 no. 1, (2010), 501–507.

4. Ibid.

5. Ibid.

6. Mark R. Warren, Soo Hong, Carolyn Leung Rubin, and Phitsamay Suchitkokhong Uy. "Beyond the Bake Sale: A Community-Based Relational Approach to Parent Engagement in Schools." *Teachers College Record*, 111 no. 9, (2009), 2209–2254.

7. Julia Bryan. (2005). "Fostering Educational Resilience and Achievement in Urban Schools through School-Family Community Partnerships." Retrieved from http://digitialcommons.unomaha..edu/slcepartnerships/22.

8. Warren et al., "Beyond the Bake Sale."

9. Steven B. Sheldon and Joyce L. Epstein. "Improving Student Behavior and School Discipline with Family and Community Involvement." *Education and Urban Society*, 35 no. 1, (2002), 4–26.

10. Joyce L. Epstein and Steven B. Sheldon. "Present and Accounted for: Improving Student Attendance through Family and Community Involvement." *The Journal of Educational Research*, 95 no. 5, (2002), 308–318.

11. Joseph Kahne, James O'Brien, Andrea Brown, and Therese Quinn. "Leveraging Social Capital and School Improvement: The Case of a Comprehensive Community Initiative in Chicago." *Educational Administration Quarterly*, 37, (2001), 429.

12. Mark R. Warren. (2005). "Communities and Schools: A New View of Urban Education Reform." *Harvard Educational Review*, 75 no. 2, 133–173.

13. C. J. Hurn. *The Limits and Possibilities of Schooling: An Introduction to the Sociology of Education*. (New York: Allyn & Bacon, 1985).

14. Anne Gregory and Michael B. Ripski. (2008). "Adolescent Trust in Teachers: Implications for Behavior in the High School Classroom." *School Psychology Review*, 37 no. 3, 337–353.

15. Russell J. Skiba and Reece L. Peterson. "School Discipline at a Crossroads: From Zero Tolerance to Early Response." *Exceptional Children*, 66 no. 3, (2000), 335–346.

16. Alison Cook-Sather (2002). "Authorizing Students' Perspectives: Toward Trust, Dialogue, and Change in Education." *Educational Researcher*, 31 no. 4, (2002), 3–14.

17. Dimitri Van Maele and Mieke Van Houtte. "The Quality of School Life: Teacher-Student Trust Relationships and the Organizational School Context." *Social Indicators Research*, 100, (2011), 85–100.

Chapter 14

Building the School to Society Pipeline

Mass Education, Not Mass Incarceration

There is a stark fact in the United States that begs to be addressed in a meaningful way: Blacks and Hispanics are always vastly overrepresented in America's prisons. Though some public attention is paid to this reality, it is often used to promote the self-fulfilling prophecy of cultural deprivation, and suggested as yet more evidence that the black and Hispanic communities, especially those in socioeconomically challenged areas, need control and containment more than anything else.

However, this is a conclusion that can only be drawn if one starts the analysis in the middle. That is, while it is not an exaggeration to claim that crime, of both the violent and nonviolent type, is rampant in socioeconomically challenged black and Hispanic communities, it is inaccurate to claim that the cause of this is based on internal cultural deficiencies or deprived cultural values.

Representing one of the most controversial discussions in contemporary American society, an earnest investigation of sociopolitical history can lead an honest and earnest student to only one conclusion: there is a deep, systematic, institutionally sanctioned (though largely tacit) tradition of black and Hispanic marginalization, which has created and caused the abject condition of their communities and its subsequent poverty and crime. Though evidencing the true intentionality of this marginalization extends the scope of the current discussion, it will be sufficient to say that, intentionally or accidentally, the American system of government and its direct and residual social practices has, and continues to systematically marginalize non-white individuals, especially those who are black and Hispanic.

Perhaps one of the most contributive elements of this repressive and oppressive system is that of the practices involving criminal justice, especially as it is applied to the non-white youth of America. As Tonry laments:

We live in a repressive era when punishment policies that would be unthinkable in other times and places are not only commonplace but also are enthusiastically supported by public officials, policy intellectuals, and much of the general public. . . . For a civil society, the United States has adopted justice policies that reflective people should abhor and that informed observers from other Western countries do abhor. [1]

Essentially, the United States, over the past three to four decades, has established a series of policies of social control with the primary component being punitive justice for all criminal offenses, the most common of which is mass incarceration. Indeed, the United States incarcerates its citizens over seven times as much as other Western countries, with the closest being the United Kingdom, over which the United States incarcerates nearly six times as many pupils per 100,000.[2]

Undoubtedly these policies have been of harsher and direr consequence to black Americans as well as Hispanics, and this clearly unequal treatment before the law has deepened an already fragile and precarious relationship between the members of these communities and the justice system.[3,4] This system has been equally as harsh to those nonviolent offenders, especially those offenses involving drugs, as it has on the violent offenders.

It is essential to note, however, that the unequal treatment of Blacks (and Hispanics, once the population became significant enough) and Whites is not unprecedented. As A. Leon Higginbotham suggested, a perception of the inferiority of the Blacks in the American justice system has functioned in order to

presume, protect and defend the ideal of superiority of whites and the inferiority of blacks. In application, this precept has not remained fixed and unchanged. Nonetheless, it has persisted even to recent times, when many of the formal, overt barriers of racism have been delegitimized.[5]

These precepts come into practice under the guise of suspicion, in which law enforcement presumes that a crime has been committed before it has been determined. As but one of many examples, sociologist Alice Goffman, in her catalyzing book *On the Run*, describes the relatively common practice of young black men avoiding medical treatment since they could be investigated by the hospital or any present law enforcement official without cause and, as a result, be detained or arrested for any prior offenses or warrants; while not without critique, Goffman clearly delineates the general suspicion which is cast upon the entire black community and the risk posed by simply living in it.[6]

The only possible result for a system such as this is one of mistrust, perceptions of illegitimacy, and presumption of unjust treatment in the eyes of its clearest victims. As Bobo and Thompson summarize:

Without asserting direct and overt racial discrimination by police, the courts, or other law enforcement agencies . . . [there are] a set of contemporary law enforcement practices and policies that are seen as unfair by design in the eyes of most Black Americans. These practices have resulted not only in the vastly disproportionate incarceration of African Americans, but also now threaten the all-important legitimacy and claim to fairness that should be the hallmark of legal institutions in a democratic society. A legal system seen as illegitimate is a system likely to face suspicion, guardedness, and even open resistance and challenge from important segments of the citizenry.[7]

Indeed, the numbers appear to support these assertions with little room for debate. According to a report presented to the United Nations in 2013 by an advocacy organization that calls itself "The Sentencing Project,"[8] it is likely that as many as one in three black males can expect to go to prison in his lifetime. More disturbing, according to an analysis of the 2010 Census, while Blacks make up only 13 percent of the entire US population, they represent more than 40 percent of the prison population (that is as compared to whites who make up 64% of the population and only 39% of the prison population; and Hispanics who make up 16% of the population and 19% of the prison population).[9]

The problem does not remain in the area of overrepresentation in terms of an academic discussion of disproportionality. Rather, the true consequences of such discriminatory practices lie in the effect on the families that are left behind, some of which leave many children without fathers, mothers or, in some cases, both. The consequences are numerous, and all contribute to the general unhealthy and unstable state of the black and Hispanic communities in which the families of convicted and incarcerated criminals remain. Some studies suggest that teens from homes with father absences (many of whose absence may be due to incarceration) are more likely to become incarcerated themselves.[10]

Other studies show clearly that black and Hispanic children are far more likely to have at least one incarcerated parent than white children, resulting in a vastly higher percentage of single-parent (or surrogate parent) homes in the black and Hispanic community. This rate of incarceration also affects foster care caseloads, resulting in the loss of quality care, sufficient supervision, and meaningful oversight in the social services field.[11] Furthermore, it is likely that the children themselves experience or directly witness a number of components of the judicial process including arrest, trial, incarceration and release, all of which can be extensively emotionally traumatizing and have lasting effects on the children's perception of the justice system itself.

These unpropitious effects on the family have an even larger cumulative effect on the community itself. Because of the clearly disproportionate concentration of mass incarceration for black and Hispanic people, the criminalization process has tended to be concentrated in these particular geographic areas. This omnipresence of law enforcement deepens the already significant mistrust in the justice system, fragmenting the already potentially unstable foundation of such neighborhoods' social systems, networks, and organizations.

Such symptoms include the weakening of family formation, tenuous labor force attachments, and general deleterious patterns of social behavior among inhabitants of the community, all of which have a deleterious effect on social capital.[12] As Elijah Anderson writes in his memoir about the steady element of criminalization in his community and its distinct deleterious effects:

> Surrounded by violence and by indifference to the innocent victims of drug dealers and users alike, the decent people are finding it harder and harder to maintain a sense of community. Thus violence comes to regulate life in the drug-infested neighborhoods and the putative neighborhood leaders are increasingly the people who control the violence.[13]

The result is a veritable mob rule, where the leaders that once sought community and growth are overthrown by those who prefer violence and power and who, in certain senses, offer more protection and economic security to the general citizens than the honest leaders before them.

The question remains, however, what does school and schooling have to do with the treatment of crimes committed in black and Hispanic communities? In what has become a significant enough social phenomenon to gain the moniker the "school to prison pipeline," it becomes glaringly obvious that schools in socioeconomically challenged black and Hispanic neighborhoods, instead of providing a safe alternative to incarceration for its youth, are actually one of the main contributories to the justice system at both the juvenile and the adult levels.

In what is a result of an unprecedented convergence between school disciplinary procedures and the judicial system, the establishment of so-called zero tolerance policies mandate that problems which occur in school be transferred to the judicial system rather than be dealt with internally.[14] Essentially, zero tolerance policies criminalize what were formerly seen as relatively minor behavioral infractions, such as petty theft and small fights, as well as more significant (and legitimately criminal) occurrences such as assaults, weapons possession, and drug-based offenses.[15]

What is most important to recognize about the school to prison pipeline is that it mirrors, as schools often do, the general trend in the greater society. That is, infractions of rules do not lead to rehabilitation or legitimate penitence (as do community service endeavors); rather they lead to harsh punitive consequences, including incarceration in either juvenile or adult facilities. As Heitzeg suggests:

The school to prison pipeline does not exist in a vacuum. It is deeply connected to a sociopolitical climate that is increasingly fearful and punitive. The tendency toward criminalization and incarceration has seeped into the schools, and with each year, this legal net ensnares younger and younger children. School funding declines precipitously, while funding for enhanced security measures rises. Behavior that once resulted in a trip to the principal's office now is grounds for a trip to jail. The willingness of some officials to have handcuffed 5 year olds escorted from school by uniformed police officers cannot be accounted for by educational policy alone.[16]

The criminalization of school misbehavior, however, is not simply a by-product of a growing social trend. There is, indeed, a clear methodology and intentionality to its practice that is revealed under closer scrutiny. Hirschfield suggests that there are three critical dimensions of school criminalization.

The first is that school punishment has become more formal, accompanied by uniform guidelines of disciplinary procedure. This leaves no room for the consideration of potentially mitigating factors such as first offenses, difficult home situations, or instances of legitimate disability such as emotional or behavioral neurological conditions. Such uniformity prevents individualization of response, and creates a veritable "criminal class" in schools.

The second is that disciplinary discretion has been transferred from teachers and school authorities to these uniform disciplinary codes. This has led to an unprecedented increase in suspensions and expulsions, sending a clear message of exclusion, as well as providing no alternative means for the individual to access support or gain a functional alternative to school attendance.

The third is the importation of a punitive criminal justice mentality in schools. Pervasive examples include law enforcement technology such as metal detectors and drug dogs, methodologies such as criminal interrogation tactics, search and seizure, and detainment, and the increased presence of criminal justice personnel, such as "school police," traditional uniformed police officers, and other punitively threatening presences such as "crisis intervention teams."[17]

With this practice comes the conveyance of a clear expectation of schoolchildren, especially those who are black and Hispanic and attend such schools. For children as young as five and six to be required to pass through metal detectors and police searches before they enter their school is not a safety measure, nor is it an effort to make schools safer. It is an effort to criminalize youth before they are even old enough to know what crime is, and to send the loud and clear message that they are, and ever will be, under suspicion. According to Stein:

> Underlying this assault on juvenile justice is the demonization of youth, particularly young people of color, who are stereotypically portrayed as roaming the streets and destroying the fabric of society. . . . The media's imagery reflects

confused reporting of crime statistics, at best, and forsakes the reality of crime rates in favor of sensationalized accounts of youthful offenders, at worst.[18]

These stereotypes, exacerbated by sensationalized accounts in the media, have a distinct effect on how teachers and administrators view young black and Hispanic children. As the facilitation of trust has been shown to be essential in the success of a school, having effects on both academic achievement as well as social and emotional well-being, the constant negative imagery against which black and Hispanic children are forced to perpetually resist results in an exhausting if not, in some cases, entirely unwinnable situation. Indeed, some studies show that young black and Hispanic children are so aware of their preconceived negative image that explicit attempts to eradicate it has comprised much of their schooling experience.[19]

ALTERNATIVES TO MASS INCARCERATION

It is inarguably clear that the recent trend in mass incarceration has little, if anything, to do with an actual increase in criminal activity, but can rather be explained by the criminalization of and consequences for activities that were once handled by very different channels and in very different ways within the educational system itself. It is further clear that there must be a change to this practice or there can be no solution to the systemic dismantling and pervasive dissolution of black and Hispanic communities, making any form of true democratic function a distinct impossibility.

While attempts to find alternatives to mass incarceration are not new, there remains relatively small interest and ostensibly low support in public policy and discourse. What support these efforts have received are generally translated into providing such programs into the technocratic functioning of the criminal justice system's existing massive bureaucracy, providing little, if any actual improvement or social difference.

An early example of this was a publication released by the Prison Research Education Action Project (PREAP) in 1976, titled *Instead of Prisons*. Naming the system "alternatives-to-incarceration" (ATI), the authors suggested that there needed to be "programs or procedures that move away from the notion of imprisonment as a response to law-breaking."[20] As Weissman conceptualizes the main difficulty with ATI was that

> while ATI programming holds promise as part of a criminal justice reform strategy, the full realization of this promise is thwarted by the structure and rules of the criminal justice system itself. More importantly, the legacy of racism in the US and the economic restructuring and abandonment of inner cities,

accompanied by an ensuing crisis in employment, fuels the push for mass incarceration as the primary response to crime.[21]

Essentially, while it may be obvious to critically minded scholars and citizens that mass incarceration is a failure as a method of social control, it is likely seen as an efficient means of social containment, lessening the dependence of challenged communities on government assistance, while relieving the already crowded workforce of a significant number of applicants and increasing general "safety." Without a fundamental shift in the paradigms that frame how both race and criminal justice are to work, this preoccupation with mass incarceration will continue to be seen as a justified response. In terms of future successes for alternatives to mass incarceration, there are a number of elements that are seen as essential for any success to be garnered, as further suggested by Weissman.[22]

The mechanics of the criminal justice system must be better designed to be more effective at gatekeeping. That is, ATIs must become better equipped to provide prevention services to those who are likely to become incarcerated. With evidence pointing directly at youth with incarcerated parents, a likely place of importance is within the school itself. That is, prevention programs in schools should not be focused on "tightening" security by raising penalties for infractions as well as "catching" potential actors through surveillance and ethically questionable searches. Rather, educational programs, alternative environments, family support mechanisms, and community building opportunities must be directly provided, and tied to, daily school functioning.

Racial disparity, including the explicit targeting of minority communities and the presumption of criminal activity must also be directly addressed. Schoolchildren should not have to bear the burden of their "race" for crimes that they did not commit, nor for the seemingly insoluble situation that their communities find themselves in. By propagating a culture of suspicion and continuing to require massive amounts of youth to attend prison-like schools, the incessant message of devaluation and mistrust will continue. The racial disparities that plague the criminal justice system are the same that plague the educational system; and it stands to reason that because the school is the main tributary to incarceration, adjusting the educational system toward a fairer form of justice will disrupt the very system itself, contributing directly to the amelioration of the injustice.

Clearly, there must also be better advocacy for ATI options at sentencing hearings at both the juvenile and the adult levels. With recidivism being as significant as it is, preventing entrance into jail to begin with is quite likely to reduce the chances of future incarceration. Elements such as wraparound planning,[23] stronger school programs that focus on academics,[24] mediation and conferencing,[25] among others are imperative components to an alternative program. With research supporting ATI programs, the influence of skilled and persuasive advocates cannot be overstated, and can create a true impact on the problem of mass incarceration, especially for the vulnerable youth of these communities.

Perhaps the most critical aspect is the forging of critical alliances within the community itself. Because mass incarceration so deeply fragments the economic, social, and cultural infrastructure of the community, fostering deeper connections between community members is likely to reduce crime, or even the ideation of crime. Allowing resources to be more readily available in these communities, combined with increased social capital and connection to the community, residents are more likely to act in the service of preservation and prosperity, rather than maintaining a tenuous, if even existent connection with their communities. Forms of such community connection can be peer-delivered services, information sharing, job support, and supporting local organizing efforts that challenge discriminatory criminal justice practices.

NOTES

1. Michael Tonry. "Rethinking Unthinkable Punishment Policies in America." *UCLA Law Review*, 46 no. 4, (1999), 1751–1791.

2. Bruce Western and Christopher Wildeman. "Punishment, Inequality, and the Future of Mass Incarceration." *Kansas Law Review*, 57, (2009), 852–877.

3. Lawrence D. Bobo and Victor Thomspon. (2006). "Unfair by Design: The War on Drugs, Race, and the Legitimacy of the Criminal Justice System." *Social Research*, 73 no. 2, (2006), 445–472.

4. Russell Skiba et al. "Race is Not Neutral: An Investigation of African American and Latino Disproportionality in School Discipline." *School Psychology Review*, 40 no. 1, (2011), 85–107.

5. Higginbotham, 1996, as cited by Bobo and Lawrence, "Unfair by Design."

6. Alice Goffman. *On the Run: Fugitive Life in an American City*. (Chicago, IL: University of Chicago Press, 2014).

7. Bobo and Thomspon, "Unfair by Design," 449.

8. http://www.sentencingproject.org/template/page.cfm?id=2.

9. Leah Sakala (2014). "Breaking Down Mass Incarceration in the 2010 Census: State-by-State Incarcerate Rates by Race/Ethnicity." Retrieved from http://www.prisonpolicy.org/reports/rates.html.

10. Cynthia S. Harper and Sara S. McLanahan. "Father Absence and Youth Incarceration." *Journal of Research on Adolescence*, 14 no. 3, (2004), 369–397.

11. Christopher Wildeman. "Parental Imprisonment, the Prison Boom, and the Concentration of Childhood Disadvantage." *Demography*, 46 no. 2, (2009), 265–280.

12. James P. Lynch and William J. Sabol. "Assessing the Effects of Mass Incarceration on Informal Social Control in Communities." *Criminology and Public Policy*, 3 no. 2, (2004), 267–293.

13. Elijah Anderson (1999). *Code of the Street: Decency, Violence, and the Moral Life of the Inner City.* (New York: Norton, 1999).

14. Nancy A. Heitzeg (2009). "Education or Incarceration: Zero Tolerance Policies and the School to Prison Pipeline." *Forum on Public Policy.* From http://files.eric.ed.gov/fulltext/EJ870076.pdf.

15. Russell Skiba and Kimberly Knesting. "Zero Tolerance, Zero Evidence: An Analysis of School Disciplinary Practice." *New Directions in Youth Development,* 92, (2001), 17–43.

16. Ibid.

17. Paul J. Hirschield. "Preparing for Prison? The Criminalization of Discipline in the USA." *Theoretical Criminology,* 12 no. 1, (2008), 79–101.

18. Stein, Nancy. "The Gang Truce: A Movement for Social Justice." *Social Justice,* 12 no. 1, 1997. From https://www.questia.com/library/journal/1G1-20562421/the-gang-truce-a-movement-for-social-justice.

19. Tyrone C. Howard. "Who Really Cares? The Disenfranchisement of African American Males in PreK-12 Schools: A Critical Race Theory Perspective." *Teachers College Record,* 110 no. 5, (2008), 954–985.

20. Marsha Weissman. "Aspiring to the Impracticable: Alternatives to Incarceration in the Era of Mass Incarceration." *NYU Review of Law & Social Change,* 33, (2009), 235–269.

21. Ibid., 237.

22. Ibid.

23. Michael D. Pullman, Jodi Kerbs, Nancy Koroloff, Ernie Veach-White, Rita Gaylor, and DeDe Sieler. "Juvenile Offenders with Mental Health Needs: Reducing Recidivism Using Wraparound." *Crime & Delinquency,* 52 no. 3, (2006), 375–397.

24. Antonis Katsiyanis, Joseph Ryan, Dalun Zhang, and Anastasia Spann. "Juvenile Delinquency and Recidivism: The Impact of Academic Achievement." *Reading & Writing Quarterly,* 24 no. 2, (2008), 177–196.

25. William Bradshaw and David Roseborough. "Restorative Justice Dialogue: The Impact of Mediation and Conferencing on Juvenile Recidivism." *Federal Probation,* 69 no. 2, (2005), 15–21.

Chapter 15

The Parameters of Earnestness

Essential Elements for True Change

While the previous chapters took a deep look into a number of crucial issues to be reckoned with if any real change is to come of education reform, this chapter draws the conversation back to the fundamentals. That is, with the specific issues and topics for change being delineated and analyzed, the final element of the conversation must turn to what the qualities of the discussion and analysis itself must be.

In an environment that has become saturated with superficial modes of accountability, "seeing is believing" mentality, and a general ignorance of history and social practice, either intentional or not, the conversation and practices resulting from it have become viciously circular. The interference of politicians, policymakers, the social elite, and corporate interests, none of which has any genuine stake in the betterment of education as a social cause, has entirely derailed the earnest conversation, and has since taken it hostage from the real stakeholders.

RESPECTING THE TRUE MULTIFACETED NATURE OF EDUCATION REFORM

The first element that must be addressed by those fully engaged in an earnest discussion of reform is that addressing the education problem is by no means a matter of simple accountability that can be resolved with better "corporate-style" management. While businesses are, indeed, concerned with regulating quality and efficiency for the most cost-effective means of turning out a "product," schools must not be regarded in such a mechanistic way. Children are not chattel, and knowledge and love of learning is not a product in any sense of the concept. It is absolutely essential for all members of the discussion to accept the fact, either by trust or by the acknowledgment of the truth that education, and all of its elements, is a result of a complex set of multiple interactions that are influenced, informed, and regulated by a number of social factors both within and outside of the school.

The general de-emphasis on the complexity of schooling forces those at the helm of policymaking to look toward quick fixes that can be "bought" or "manufactured," and then superimposed on a human relationship-based system; as a consequence, failure to produce change at a steady enough rate, at least in terms of the metric of change being used (such as standardized testing) immediately warrants further action. This is simply not the way that human organizations or human learning works.

The process of learning has been horrifyingly oversimplified, and those who adopt a business-model approach to schooling in terms of both process and "product" will never be satisfied with any true reform. Further, any reform that simply enhances test scores is not indicative of legitimate reform or meaningful change at all, but rather a means of learning how to manipulate the instrument itself for desired results; essentially no more than a self-fulfilling prophecy.

Discussions about school change must focus on all of the issues mentioned in the preceding chapters, as well as any other issues that come to light, or ways in which the acknowledged issues change in and of themselves. Schooling will remain the most important public venture, but also most elusive, being both reflective of and receptive to any number of changes in social, political, and economic variations that will ever face a nation as large, diverse and globally significant as the United States.

ALLOWING TIME FOR CHANGE AND FOR REAL DIALOGUE

In a society that has become deeply impatient and dependent on immediacy, especially given the challenge of technology providing information from all types of media in seconds regardless of its accuracy, veracity, practicality, factuality, or even morality, the notion of patience for allowing change has become entirely foreign, if not demonized as passé or, worse, entirely obsolete. This impatience has permeated into the realm of public policy which, though historically has always demanded more obvious changes more quickly, has come to sabotage itself with its incessant self-counteraction in the area of educational policy. Cuban and Tyack referred to these types of policies as being "fireflies" as they are obvious and present for a moment but quickly fade, we must take this metaphor almost literally.[1] It is not the glowing that matters, but for how long it glows.

In addition to, or perhaps as a function of, providing enough time, more space needs to be provided for genuine dialogue to take place. The dialogue that does exist is largely discursive, riddled with preconceptions, distractions and diversions, preventing any meaningful conversation between parties to take place.

Indeed, there may be deep levels of disagreements that come from genuine differences in conceptions of morality, practicality, purpose of schooling, national identity, global identity, citizenship, and competitiveness, among many others. These differences will not disappear, and maintaining or reversing dominance from any of the "sides" within the group will result only in continued marginalization and discontentment. The difference will lie only in which group or groups are now relegated to the margins and those who have become dominant in its place. This result is neither productive nor democratic in nature. Rather, real discussions, perhaps formalized if necessary (i.e., providing each "participant" a certain venue, timeframe, medium, etc.) to delineate their points in whatever way necessary must be available.

It is foolish and idealistic to require that the whole of the public be actively participatory, or to assume that there is any such interest in "listening" or "engaging" on a widespread level. However, the opportunity must be available and truly accessible for any citizen or participant who would like to exercise their right of participation. Similarly, those in charge (i.e., those who hold the power in governance structure) *must* be willing to relegate as much time and space as necessary to facilitate the dialogue, as well as to be actively involved. Though they may be disinterested in the content or otherwise unconvinced, they have an obligation to their constituents who have placed them in their position by election.

Quite importantly, the issue of the teachers' union versus nonunion ideology has been among the most divisive of entities in the quest for true dialogue. While it is imprudent to cast blame on either side, as both have done already leading to nothing other than continued conflict, conflated arguments, diversion, and hostility, the issue needs to be refocused on education reform itself. That is, many people may have legitimate concerns over the role, political connectivity, or even morality of the union as an organization. These may be justified or unjustified, or based on experience or simply one's perception.

As Finland has demonstrated, the existence of a union as an entity is not, in itself, detracting to education reform, as the national union plays an active and relatively nonacrimonious function. However, the relevant and irrelevant issues must be kept separate, and multiple discussions, if necessary, must be allowed to take place at various times, some of which are immediately relevant, some of which are less so, and some of which may have little value or relevance to education reform at all despite its "existence" in the education rhetoric. Indeed, both "sides" would benefit from more structured and productive modalities to dialogue.

THE NEED FOR TRUE, ACCURATE, AND VALUABLE MEANS OF ACCOUNTABILITY

Many of the arguments involving education reform get conflated with, rightfully so at times, and unwarrantedly in others, the idea of accountability. Germane to the above discussion involving unions, a common preconception, erroneous as it is, is that teachers and teacher unions are averse to any form of accountability or evaluative measures. This is patently untrue, and can be seen as a legitimate slander against the agendas of any teacher union. Rather, what teachers and unions do sincerely oppose is the overly simplistic, entirely quantitative, and ill-equipped measures that are used to gauge their effectiveness.

While there is, and will likely always remain rhetoric in favor of the idea that teacher effectiveness can be gauged simply by their students' achievement on a test (i.e., if a teacher is effective at teaching the material, the student should perform well on the test) this characterization amounts to one of the most vicious applications of oversimplification of the teaching and learning process. The research in this area is quite clear and largely uncontradicted: scores on standardized tests are influenced as much, if not more so, by factors outside of the teachers' control than by factors within it.

An analogy may be of use for this segment of the argument. It would be hard to suggest that doctors should be unaccountable for their service and care of patients. However, it would be equally as unfair to hold entirely accountable the doctor who is overseeing the care of a lung cancer patient who has smoked for 30 years, and continues to do so throughout her treatment. The doctor can, irrefutably, manipulate and mechanize the type of treatment that the individual receives while directly under his or her care. The doctor cannot, by any means, control the individual's behavior, past, present, or future, choice-making processes, and social influences outside of direct care. This can also be said of an overweight patient with heart disease, who continues to eat poorly and refrain from exercise.

The same is true of a teacher, though in a way even more complex. While the teacher can, in some ways, control the type of material he or she uses (though in many cases materials are controlled by the larger educational entity), the condition of the classroom in which the students receive instruction (to an extent), the amount of positive engagement and care provided, among a number of other largely controllable factors, teachers cannot control the environment in which the student spends the remaining 18 odd hours of each day, and must not be held responsible for it. Factors including whether a child is abused, malnourished, ill-cared for, left home alone, helped with homework, does homework at all, among a number of other significant contributors to school performance is far beyond the teacher's control, though will unequivocally have a significant effect on a test score.

The assumption of current educational reform, especially in light of using standardized testing to evaluate the effectiveness of teachers and achievement of students, clearly disregards the above realities despite the availability of vast and convincing research support.[2] Most disregarded, however, is the means of assessment itself.

Generally conceptualized as "value-added assessment," the current means of evaluating the effectiveness of teachers as a statistical function of student scores on standardized tests has become the norm for many states' teacher evaluation systems, quite clearly as a result of the stipulations for such systems in Race to the Top applications. However, in and of itself, value-added measurement, while shown to be useful in certain areas of social science for investigating particular types of questions, is far too precarious and imprecise to be confidently used to evaluate teacher effectiveness, especially when such measures can be factored into personnel decisions.[3,4]

An equally relevant question, however, is how the use of standardized tests affects students in terms of both gauging academic achievement as well as affecting mental health. Research supports the notion that emotional regulation is a significant predictor of academic performance, and emotional states such as anxiety can be significantly exacerbated during assessment-based activities such as high-stakes testing.[5,6,7] This becomes especially true when considering students with various types of learning challenges, such as specific learning disabilities, language difficulties, and even nonnative speakers of English.[8]

What then, should the role of testing be? While many would argue, in some ways compellingly, to eliminate the use of standardized tests altogether, this is not a necessary measure. Rather, providing for more versatile, comprehensive, qualitative, and reflective means of accounting for teacher practice as well as student growth is an absolute necessity. Standardized testing could provide very important information on both of these elements, but must not remain the sole metric, or the most valued metric used.[9] There is no question that the current focus on testing is driven entirely by the corporate interest in public schools, and it has created nothing but a burden for teachers, students and parents alike. Teaching should not and must not be reduced to a score, as is also the case with student learning. This is another lesson the United States should, but fails, to take from Finland.

MINIMIZING THE INFLUENCE OF CORPORATIZATION
IN PUBLIC SCHOOLING

It is argued that the most likely source for all of the above mentioned difficulties in meaningful education reform is corporatization. It is virtually inarguable that there can be no other interest in corporatizing public schools than profiteering. The close investigation of the incestuous relationships between corporations, both within and outside of the United States, and schools is glaringly obvious, and the nearly ubiquitous financial benefits for a corporation to become involved in the schooling "industry" bears even more evidence. This is the apex of the immorality of a neoliberal system (though one that also benefits a conservative system as well), and threatens, more deeply than anything else, the functioning of a truly democratic system.

The deep influence that the corporate testing industry has had on the creation, "validation," and implementation on the Common Core State Standards (CCSS) is unmistakable, and the resulting stake it has on the companies that are to profit from the curricular materials is even more glaring. For a policy practice in a purportedly democratic country to hinge so deeply on the availability of corporate products, much of which was (and is) paid for by public monies, is an affront to democracy itself.[10]

How then does the public school system separate itself from corporatization? Further, what role, if any, can and should corporate entities play in public school functioning? It would be foolish to suggest that in a devoutly capitalist country corporate entities can play no role. Indeed, it may be equally as foolish to claim that they should not. Most certainly, the products they provide are widely available, often engaging, sometimes effective, and most likely time-saving for teachers who are pressed for preparatory time to begin with.

Therefore, the elimination of the availability of commercial educational materials is neither a rational nor a productive step. Rather, the role that these companies play should be provisional in nature, and the competition should be rooted between the private companies themselves, not between entities of the public itself, such as traditional public schools with traditionally available budgets competing with corporate-backed charter schools with vastly more resources. For tests to be created, sold, distributed, and scored entirely under the auspice of one or two companies in a "state-sponsored" venture is entirely undemocratic, especially when there is a likelihood that officials within that governance system have personal financial interests in those companies.[11,12,13]

NOTES

1. Tyack and Cuban, *Tinkering toward Utopia*.

2. Dale Ballou, William Sanders and Paul Wright. "Controlling for Student Background inValue-Added Assessment." *Journal of Educational and Behavioral Statistics*, 29 no. 1, (2004), 37–65.

3. Harold C. Doran and Steve Fleischman. "Challenges of Value-Added Assessment." *Educational Leadership*, 63 no. 3, (2005), 85–87.

4. McCaffrey, Daniel F., J.R. Lockwood, Daniel M. Koretz, and Laura S. Hamilton. (2004)."Evaluating Value-Added Models for Teacher Accountability." From https://www.rand.org/content/dam/rand/pubs/monographs/2004/RAND_MG158.pdf.

5. Mark H. Ashcraft and Alex M. Moore. "Mathematics Anxiety and the Affective Drop in Performance." *Journal of Psychoeducational Assessment*, 27 no. 3, (2009), 197–205.

6. Reinhard Pekrum, Andrew J. Elliot, and Markus A. Meier. "Achievement Goals and Achievement Emotions: Testing a Model of Their Joint Relations with Academic Performance." *Journal of Educational Psychology*, 101 no. 1, (2009), 115–135.

7. Paulo A. Graziano, Rachael D. Reavis, Susan P. Keane, and Susan D. Calkins. "The Role of Emotion Regulation and Children's Early Academic Success." *Journal of School Psychology*, 45 no. 1, (2007), 3–19.

8. Spencer J. Salend. "Addressing Test Anxiety." *Teaching Exceptional Children*, 44 no. 2, (2011), 58–68.

9. Caldas, Stephen J. "The Emperor with No Clothes." *Educational Leadership,* 70 no. 3, 2012. From http://www.ascd.org/publications/educational-leadership/current-issue.aspx.

10. Susan Ohanian. "Gates Financed Common Core Standards Turned Kindergarten into Global Economy Zone." Retrieved from http://www.dailycensored.com/gates-financed-common-core-standards-turn-kindergarten-into-global-economy-zone/.

11. Editorial.(2015)."TischMustStepAside."Retrievedfromhttp://www.lohud.com/story/opinion/editorials/2015/04/19/tisch-must-step-aside/26026693/.

12. http://unitedoptout.com/2012/04/27/boycott-pearson-now/.

13. Michelle Malkin (2015) "Jeb Bush, Common Core Cronie$, Pearson, PARCC, and Your Kids' Privacy." Retrieved from http://michellemalkin.com/2015/03/18/jeb-bush-common-core-cronie-pearson-parcc-and-your-kids-privacy/.

Bibliography

Adams, John. (1776). "Thoughts on Government." From http://www.constitution.org/jadams/thoughts.htm.

Adams, John. (1775). "Letter from John Adams to Abigail Adams, 29 October 1775." From http://www.masshist.org/digitaladams/archive/doc?id=L17751029jathird.

Allen, Ricky Lee. "Whiteness and Critical Pedagogy." *Educational Philosophy and Theory*, 36 no. 2, 2004: 121–136.

Ashcraft, Mark H. and Alex Moore. "Mathematics Anxiety and the Affective Drop in Performance." *Journal of Psychoeducational Assessment*, 27 no. 3, 2009: 197–205.

Americans for Tax Fairness. From http://www.americansfortaxfairness.org/tax-fairness-briefing-booklet/fact-sheet-corporate-tax-rates

Anderson, Elijah. *Code on the Street: Decency, Violence, and the Moral Life of the Inner City.* New York: Norton, 1999.

Ascher, Carol. "Performance Contracting: A Forgotten Experiment in School Privatization." *Phi Delta Kapan*, 77 no. 9: 615.

Astiz, M. Fernanda, Alexander Wiseman, and David P. Baker. "Slouching Toward-Decentralization: Consequences of Globalization for Curricular Control in National Education Systems." *Comparative Education Review*, 46 no. 1, 2002: 66–88.

Au, Wayne. "What's a Nice Test Like You Doing in a Place Like This? The edTPA and Corporate Education Reform." *Rethinking Schools,* 13 no. 4 2013. From http://www.rethinkingschools.org/archive/27_04/27_04_au.shtml

Ballou, Dale, William Sanders and Paul Wright. "Controlling for Student Background in Value-Added Assessment." *Journal of Educational and Behavioral Statistics*, 29 no. 1, 2004: 37–65.

Banks, James A. "Diversity, Group Identity, and Citizenship Education in a Global Age." *Educational Researcher*, 37 no. 3, 2008: 129–139.

Bartlett, Lesley, Maria Frederick, Thadeus Gulbrandsen, and Enrique Murillo. "The Marketization of Education: Public Schools for Private Ends. *Anthorpology & Education Quarterly,* 33 no. 1, 2002: 1–25.

Bascia, Nina and Pamela Osmond. (2012). Teacher Unions and Educational Reform: A Research Review. National Education Association Center for Great Public Schools Research Department: From https://feaweb.org/_data/files/ED_Reform/Teacher_Unions_and_Educational_Reform.pdf

Berman, Sheldon. *Children's Social Consciousness and the Development of Social-Responsibility*. Albany, NY: SUNY Press, 1997.

Bifulco, Robert and Helen F. Ladd. "School Choice, Racial Segregation, and Test-Score Gaps: Evidence from North Carolina's Charter School Program." *Journal of Policy Analysis and Management*, 26 no. 1, 2007: 31–56.

Bifulco, Robert, Helen Ladd, and Stephen L. Ross. "Public School Choice and Integration Evidence from Durham, North Carolina." *Social Science Research,* 38 no 1. 2009. 71–85.

Bobo, Lawrence D. and Victor Thompson. "Unfair by Design: The War on Drugs, race, and the Legitimacy of the Criminal Justice System." *Social Research*, 73 no. 2, 2006: 445–472.

Bosma, Linda M., Renee E. Sieving, Annie Ericson, Pamela Russ, Laura Cavender, and Mark Bonne. "Elements for a Successful Collaboration Between K-12 School, Community, and University Partners: The Lead Peace Partnership. *Journal of School Health*, 80 no. 1, 2010: 501–507.

Bradshaw, William and David Roseborough. "Restorative Justice Dialogue: The Impact of Mediation and Conferencing on Juvenile Recidivism." *Federal Probation*, 69 no. 2, 2005: 15–21.

Brown, Dave F. "Urban Teachers' Professed Classroom Management Strategies: Reflections of Culturally Responsive Teaching." *Urban Education*, 39 no. 3, 2204: 266–289.

Brown, Monica R. "Educating All Students: Creating Culturally Responsive Teachers,Classrooms, and Schools." *Intervention in School and Clinic*, 43, 2007: 57.

Bryan, Julia. (2005). "Fostering Educational Resilience and Achievement in Urban Schools Through School-Family Community Partnerships." From http://digitalcommons.unomaha.edu/cgi/viewcontent.cgi?article=1019&context=slcepartnerships

Bryk, Anthony S. and Barbara Schneider. "Trust in Schools: A Core Resource for School Reform." *Educational Leadership*, 60 no. 6, 2003: 40–45.

Cabannes, Yves. "Participatory Budgeting: A Significant Contribution to Participatory Democracy." *Environment & Urbanization*, 16 no. 1, 2004: 27–46.

Caldas, Stephen J. "The Emperor with No Clothes." *Educational Leadership,* 70 no. 3, 2012. From http://www.ascd.org/publications/educational-leadership/current-issue.aspx.

Carnoy, Martin, Rebecca Jacobsen, Lawrence Mishel, and Richard Rothstein. "The Charter School Dust Up." Washington, D.C.: Economic Policy Institute, 2005.

Chubb, John E. and Terry M. Moe. *Politics, Markets, and America's Schools*. Washington, D.C.: Brookings Institution Press, 1990.

Clarke, Prema. "Culture and Classroom Reform: The Case of the District Primary Education Project, India." *Comparative Education*, 39 no. 1, 27–44.

Cook-Sather, Alison. "Authorizing Students' Perspectives: Toward Trust, Dialogue, and Change in Education." *Educational Researcher*, 31 no. 4, 2002: 3–14.

Crosby, Emeral A. "Urban Schools Forced to Fail." *Phi Delta Kappan*, 81 no. 4, 1999: 298–303.

Cruse, Kevin M. *One Nation Under God*. New York: Basic Books, 2015.

Cunnifee, Eileen. (2014) "Wait—What is Venture Philanthropy Again?" *Nonprofit Quarterly*. From https://nonprofitquarterly.org/2014/03/12/wait-what-is-venture-philanthropy-again.

Darling-Hammond, L., Deborah J. Holtzman, Su Jin Gatlin, and Julian Vasquez Heilig. (2005). "Does Teacher Preparation Matter? Evidence about Teacher Certification, Teach for America, and Teacher Effectiveness." *Educational Analysis Policy Archives*, 13 no. 42. From file:///C:/Users/eshyman/Downloads/147-436-1-PB.pdf

DiAngelo, Robin. "White Fragility." *International Journal of Critical Pedagogy*, 3 no. 3, 2011: 54–70.

Doran, Harold C. and Steve Fleischman. "Challenges of Value-Added Assessment." *Educational Leadership*, 63 no. 3, 2005: 85–87.

Editorial. (2015). "Tisch Must Step Aside." From http://www.lohud.com/story/opinion/editorials/2015/04/19/tisch-must-step-aside/26026693/

Editors. (2013). "The Trouble with the Common Core." From http://www.rethinking-schools.org/archive/27_04/edit274.shtml.

Epstein, Joyce L. and Steven B. Sheldon. "Present and Accounted For: Improving Student Attendance Through Family and Community Involvement." *The Journal of Educational Research*, 95 no. 5, 308–318.

Farley, Todd. *Making the Grades: My Misadventures in the Standardized Testing Industry*. San Francisco: Berrett-Keohler Publishers, 2009.

Feistritzer, C. Emily. (2011). "Prifles of Teachers in the U.S. 2011." National Center for Education Information. Retrieved from https://www.edweek.org/media/pot2011final-blog.pdf.

Fisher, Simon and David Hicks. *World Studies 8-13: A Teacher's Handbook*. Edinburgh, UK: Oliver & Boyd, 1985,

Frankenberg, E. and Chungmei Lee. "Charter Schools and Race: A Lost Opportunity for Integrated Education." Cambridge, MA: Harvard Civil Rights Project, 2003.

Frankenberg, E., G. Siegel Hawley, and J. Wang. "Choice Without Equity: Charter-School Segregation." *Educational Policy Analysis Archives*, 19 no. 1, 2011. From http://epaa.asu.edu/article/view/779

Freire, Paulo. *The Pedagogy of the Oppressed*. New York: Bloomsbury, 1993.

Fung, Archon and Erik Olin Wright. "Deepening Democracy: Innovations in Empowered Participatory Governance." *Politics & Society*, 29 no. 1, 2001: 5–41.

Furlong, John, Marilyn Cochran-Smith, and Marie Brennan. "Policy and Politics in Teacher Education: International Perspectives." *Teachers and Teaching: Theory and Practice*, 14 no. 4, 2008: 265–269.

Gaventa, John. "Towards a Participatory Governance: Assessing the Transformative-Possiblities." In *Participation—From Tyranny to Transformation?: Exploring New Approaches to Participation in Development*, Samuel Hickey and Giles Mohan (Eds.): London: Zed Books, 2004, 25–39.

Bibliography

Gillborn, David. "Education Policy as an Act of White Supremacy: Whiteness, Critical Race Theory, and Education Reform." *Journal of Education Policy*, 20 no. 4, 2005: 485–505.

Goffman, Alice. "On the Run: Fugitive Life in American City." Chicago: University of Chicago Press, 2014.

Good, Thomas L. and Jennifer S. Braden. *The Great School Debate: Choice, Vouchers, and Charters*. New York: Routledge, 1999.

Graziano, Paulo A., Rachael D. Reavis, Susan P. Keane, and Susan D. Calkins. "The Role of Emotion Regulation and Children's Early Academic Success." *Journal of School Psychology*, 45 no. 1, 3–19.

Gregory, Anne and Michael B. Ripski. "Adolescent Trust in Teachers: Implications for Behavior in the High School Classroom." *School Psychology Review*, 37 no. 3, 337–353.

Groom, Barry and Irmeli Maunonen-Eskelinen. "The Use of Portfolios to Develop Reflective Practice in Teacher Training: A Comparative and Collaborative Approach Between Two Teacher Training Providers in the UK and Finland." *Teaching in Higher Education*, 11 no. 3, 2006: 291–300.

Guggenheim, Davis. (2010). "Waiting for Superman." From http://www.imdb.com/title/tt1566648.

Harper, Cynthia S. and Sara S. McLanahan. "Father Absence and Youth Incarceration." *Journal of Research on Adolescence,* 14 no. 3, 2014: 369–397.

Hastings, Justine S., Thomas J. Kane, and Douglas Steiger. "Preferences and Heterogeneous Treatment Effects in a Public School Choice Lottery." From http://www.nber.org/papers/w12145.

Heitzeg, Nancy A. (2009). "Education or Incarceration: Zero Tolerance Policies and the School to Prison Pipeline." *Forum on Public Policy*. From http://files.eric.ed.gov/fulltext/EJ870076.pdf

Heller, Patrick, K.N. Harilal, and Shubdam Chaudhuri. "Building Local Democracy: Evaluating the Impact of Decentralisation in Kerala, India." *World Development*, 35 no. 4, 2007: 626–648

Henig, Jeffrey. "What Do We Know About the Outcomes of KIPP Schools?" East Lansing, MI: Great Lakes Center for Education, 2008. From http://greatlakescenter.org/docs/Policy_Briefs/Henig_Kipp.pdf

Hirschfield, Paul J. "Preparing for Prison? The Criminalization of Discipline in the USA." *Theoretical Criminology*, 12 no.1, 2008: 79–101.

Holden, Cathie. "Learning for Democracy: From World Studies to Global Citizenship." *Theory Into Practice,* 39 no. 2, 2000: 74–80.

Holme, Jennifer Jellison. "Buying Homes, Buying Schools: School Choice and the Social Construction of School Quality, *Harvard Educational Review*, 72 no. 2, 2002: 177–205.

Horvat, Erin McNamara, Elliot B. Weininger, and Annette Lareau. "From Social Ties to Social Capital: Class Differences in the Relations Between Schools and Parent Networks." *American Educational Research Review*, 40 no. 2, 2003: 319–351.

Howard, Tyrone C. "Who Really Cares? The Disenfranchisement of African American Males in PreK-12 Schools: A Critical Race Theory Perspective." *Teachers College Record*, 110 no. 5, 2008: 954–985.

Hoy, Wayne K. "Faculty Trust: A Key to Student Achievement." *Journal of School Public Relations*, 32 no. 2, 88–103.

Hoy, Wayne K. & C. John Tarter. "Organizational Justice in Schools: No Justice Without Trust." *International Journal of Educational Management*, 18 no. 4, 2004: 250–259.

Hurn, C.J. *The Limits and Possibilities of Schooling: An Introduction to the Sociology of Education*. New York: Allyn & Bacon, 1985.

Jakku-Sihvonen, Ritva, Varpu Tissari, Aivar Ots, and Satu Uusiautti. "Teacher Education Curricular after the Bologna Process—A Comparative Analysis of Written Curricula in Finland and Estonia." *Scandanavian Journal of Educational Research*, 56 no. 3, 2012: 261–275.

Jefferson, Thomas. (n.d.). *The Papers of Thomas Jefferson: Digital Edition*. From: http://rotunda.upress.virginia.edu/founders/TSJN.html.

Jefferson, Thomas. (1820). "Letter from Thomas Jefferson to William C. Jarvis." From: http://famguardian.org/Subjects/POlitics/thomasjefferson/jeff1350.htm.

Kahne, Joseph, James O'Brien, Andrea Brown, and Therese Quinn. "Leveraging Social Capital and School Improvement: The Case of a Comprehensive Community Initiative in Chicago." *Educational Administration Quarterly*, 37, 2001: 429.

Katsiyanis, Anotnis, Joseph Ryan, Dalun Zhang, and Anastasia Spann. "Juvenile Delinquency and Recidivism: The Impact of Academic Achievement." *Reading & Writing Quarterly*, 24 no. 2, 2008: 177–196.

Katz, Michael B. "The Origins of Public Education: A Reassessment." *History of Education Quarterly*, 16 no. 4, 1976: 381–407.

Kim, Pan Suk, John Halligan, Namshin Cho, CHeol H. Oh, and Angela M. Eikenberry. "Toward Participatory and Transparent Governance: report on the Sixth Global Forum on Reinventing Government." *Public Administration Review*, 65 no. 6, 2005: 647.

Klein, Alyson. (September 23, 2014). "Historic Summit Fueled Push for K-12 Standards." From http://www.edweek.org/ew/articles/2014/09/24/05summit.h34.html.

Klein, Naomi. *The Shock Doctrine*. New York: Picador, 2007.

Kliebard, Herbert M. *The Struggle for the American Curriculum 1893-1958*. New York: Routledge, 2005.

Klingner, Janette, Alfredo J. Artiles, Elizabeth Kozelski, Beth Harry, Shelley Zion, William Tate, Grace Zemora Duran, and David Riley. "Addressing the Disproportionate Representation of Special Education Through Cultural Responsive Educational Systems. *Educational Policy Analysis Archives, 13* no. 38, 2005. From http://epaa.asu.edu/ojs/article/view/143

Krzywacki, Heidi. (2009). "Becoming a Teacher: Emerging Teacher Identity in mathematics Teacher Education." From: https://helda/helsinki.fi/bitstream/handle/10138/20029

Kumashiro, Kevin. (2012). "When Billionaires Become Educational Experts." *Academe*. From http://www.aaup.org/article/when-billionaires-become-educational-experts#.VpQW62M0_x4.

Lackzo-Kerr, Ildiko and David C. Berliner. (2002). "The Effectiveness of 'Teach for America' and Other Under-Certified Teachers on Student Academic Achievement: A Case of Harmful Public Policy." *Educational Analysis Policy Archives*, 10 no. 37. From http://epaa.asu.edu/ojs/article/view/316

Ladd, Helen. "Education and Poverty: Confronting the Evidence." *Journal of Policy Analysis and Management*, 31 no. 2, 2012: 203–227.

Ladson-Billings, Gloria. "Culture Versus Citizenship: The Challenge of Racialized Citizenship in the United States." In James A. Banks (Ed.) *Diversity and Citizenship in Education: Global Perspectives.* San Francisco: Jossey-Bass.

Lerkannen, Marja-Kristiina, Eve Kikas, Eija Pakarinen, Pirjo-Liisa Poikonen, and Jari-Erik Nurmi. "Mothers' Trust Toward Teachers in Relation to Teaching Practices." *Early Childhood Research Quarterly*, 28, 2013: 153–165.

Levinson, Bradley A. "Education reform sparks Teacher Protest in Mexico." *Phi Delta Kappan*, May, 2014: 48–51.

Levitas, Toni and Jan Herczynski. (2001). "Decentralization, Local Governments, and Education Reform in Post-Communist Poland." From https://www.rti.org/pubs/levitas)LG_fiancne_reform_Poland.pdf

Leystina, Pepi. "Corporate Testing: Standards, Profits, and the Demise of the Public Sphere." *Teacher Education Quarterly,* 34 no. 2, 2007: 59–84.

Lister, Ruth. "Citizen in Action: Citizenship and Community Development in the Northern Ireland Context." *Community Development Journal*, 33 no. 3, 1998: 226–235.

Lubienski, Christopher A. and Sarah Theule Lubienski. *The Public School Advantage: Why Public Schools Outperform Private Schools.* Chicago: University of Chicago Press, 2013.

Lynch, James P. and William J. Sabol. "Assessing the Effects of Mass Incarceration on Informal Social Control in Communities." *Criminology and Public Policy*, 3 no. 2, 2004: 267–293.

Malkin, Michelle. (2015). "Jeb Bush, Common Core Cronie$, Pearson, PARCC, and Your Kids' Privacy." From http://michellemalkin.com/2015/03/18/jeb-bush-common-core-cronie-pearson-parcc-and-your-kids-privacy/

Marsh, Julie A., Ron W. Zimmer, Deanna Hill, and Brian P. Gill. "A Brief History of Edison Schools and a Review of Existing Literature." From http://www.rand.org/content/dam/rand/pubs/monographs/2005/RAND_MG351.pdf

McCaffrey, Daniel F., J.R. Lockwood, Daniel M. Koretz, and Laura S. Hamilton. (2004). "Evaluating Value-Added Models for Teacher Accountability." From https://www.rand.org/content/dam/rand/pubs/monographs/2004/RAND_MG158.pdf

Metcalf, Stephen. (2002). "Reading Between the Lines." *The Nation.* From http://www.thenation.com/article/reading-between-lines.

Minnesota State Legislature. From http://www.leg.state.mn.us/lrl/issues/issues?issue=charter

Miron, Gary, Jessica Urschel, William J. Mathis, and Elana Tornquist. (2010). "Schools Without Diversity: Educational Management Organizations, Charter Schools, and Demographic Stratification of the American School System. Education and the Public Interest Center & Education Policy Research Unit. From http://epicpolicy.org/publication/schools-without-diversity.

Mondale, Sarah. *School: The Story of American Public Education.* New York: Beacon, 2002.

Mora, Richard and Mary Chistianakis. "Charter Schools, Market Capitalism, and Obam'as Neo-liberal Agenda." *Journal of Inquiry & Action*, 4 no. 1, 2011: 93–111.

Mulikottu-Veetill and Mark Brady. "The Decentralisation on Education in Kerala State, India: Rhetoric and Reality." *International Review of Education,* 50, 2004: 223–243.

Myers, J.P. "Rethinking Social Studies Curriculum in the Context of Globalization: Education for Global Citizenship in the U.S." *Theory and Research in Social Education,* 34 no. 3, 2006: 370–394.

Nathan, Joseph. "Heat and Light in the Charter School Movement." *Phi Delta Kappan,* 79 no. 7: 499–505.

Nathan, Joseph. *Charter Schools: Creating Hope and Opportunity for American Education.* San Francisco: Jossey-Bass, 1996.

Nation at Risk. From http://www2.ed.gov/pubs/NatAtRisk/risk.html.

National Education Association. From http://www.nea.org/home/46665.htm

National Governors Association. From http:www.nga.org/cms/home/news-room/news-releases

Noguera, Pedro. "Social Capital and the Education of Immigrant Students." *Sociology of Education,* 77 no. 2, 2004: 180–183.

NYS Allies for Public Education. From http://www.nysape.org/allies.html

Ohanian, Susan. (2013). "Gates Financed Common Core Standards Turned Kindergarten into Global Economy Zone." From http://www.dailycensored.com/gates-financed-common-core-standards-turn-kindergarten-into-global-economy-zone/

Ohanian, Susan. (2013). "28 Questions About the Common Core." From http://vtdigger.org/2013/08/13/ohanian-28-questions-about-the-common-core.

Ohanian, Susan. *What Happened to Recess and Why Are Our Children Struggling in Kindergarten.* New York: McGraw-Hill Education, 2002.

Orfield, Gary and Erica Frankenberg. *Educational Delusions: Why Choice can Deepen Inequality and How to Make Schools Fair.* Los Angeles: University of California Press, 2013.

Ornelas, Carlos. (n.d.) "The Politics of the Educational Decentralization in Mexico." From http://citesserx.ist.psu.edu/viewdoc/download?doi=10.1.1.202.5811&rep+rep1&type-pdf.

Papay, John. (2013). "What's Driving Teachers Away From High Poverty Schools." *Center on Great Teachers & Leaders.* From http://www.gtlcenter.org/blog/what%E2%80%99s-driving-teachers-away-high-poverty-schools

Pekrum, Reinhard, Andrew J. Elliot, and Markus A. Meier. "Achievement Goals and Achievement Emotions: Testing a Model of their Joint Relations with Academic Performance." *Journal of Educational Psychology,* 101 no. 1, 115–135.

Postman, Neil. *The End of Education: Redefining the Value of School.* New York: Vintage, 1996.

Pullman, Michael D., Jodi Kerbs, Nancy Koroloff, Ernie Veach-White, Rita Gaylor, and DeDe Sieler. "Juvenile Offenders with Mental Health Needs: Reducing Recidivism Using Wraparound." *Crime & Delinquency,* 52 no. 3, 375–397.

Ravitch, Diane. *The Troubled Crusade: American Education 1945—1980.* New York: Basic Books, 1985.

Ravitch, Diane and Joseph Vitteri. *New Schools for a New Century: The Redesign of Urban Education.* New Haven, CT: Yale University Press, 1999.

Ravitch, Diane. *Reign of Error: The Hoax of the Privatization Movement and the Danger to America's Public Schools.* New York: Vintage, 2014.

Ravitch, Diane. (2014). "Public Education: Who Are the Corporate Reformers?" From http://billmoyers.com/2014/03/28/ublic-education-who-are-the-corporate-reformers/

Rawls, Kristin. (2013). "Who is Profiting from Charters? The Big Bucks Behind Charter School Secrecy, Financial Scandal, and Corruption." From http://www.alternet.org/education/who-profiting-charters-big-bucks-behind-charter-school-secrecy-financial-scandal-and

Ripley, Amanda. *The Smartest Kids in the World: And How They Got That Way.* New York: Simon & Schuster, 2014.

Sackler, Madeleine. (2010). "The Lottery." From www.thelotteryfilm.com

Sahlberg, Pasi. "Education Policies for Raising Student Learning: The Finnish Approach." *Journal of Education Policy*, 22 no. 2, 2007: 147–171.

Sahlberg, Pasi. (March 31, 2015). "Q: What Makes Finnish Teachers so Speical? A: It's Not Brains." From http://www.theguradian.com/education/2015/mar/31/finnish-teachers-special-train-teach.

Salazar Pererz, Michelle and Gaile S. Cannella. *Childhoods: A Handbook.* New York: Peter Lang, 2010.

Sakala, Leah. (2014). "Breaking Down Mass Incarceration in the 2010 Census: State-by-State Incarcerate Rates by Race/Ethnicity." From http://www.prisonpolicy.org/reports/rates/html.

Salend, Spencer J. "Addressing Test Anxiety." *Teaching Exceptional Children*, 44 no. 2, 58–68.

Saltman, Kenneth. "Putting the Public Back in Public Schooling Beyond the Corporate Model." *DePaul Journal for Social Justice*, 3 no. 1, 2009: 9–39.

Sass, Timothy R. "Charter School and Student Achievement in Florida." *Education Finance and Policy*, 1 no. 1: 91–122.

Schneider, Mercedes. (April 23, 2014). "Those 24 Common Core Work Group Memebers." From http://deutsch29.wordpress.com/2014/04/23/those-24-common-core-2009-work-group-members

Schneider, Mercedes. (April 25, 2014). A Tale of Two NGA Press Releases, and Then Some. From https://deutsch29.wordpress.com/2014/04/25/a-tale-of-two-nga-press-releases-and -then-some.

Seashore, Karen Louis. "Trust and Improvement in Schools." *Journal of Educational Change*, 8 no. 1, 2007: 1–24.

Seashore, Karen Louis. "Changing the Culture of Schools: Professional Community, Organizational Learning, and Trust." *Journal of School Leadership*, 16, 2006: 477–489.

Sheldon, Steven B. and Joyce L. Epstein. "Improving Student Behavior and School Discipline with Family and Community Involvement." *Education and Urban Society*, 35 no. 1, 2002: 4–26.

Simola, Hannu. "The Finnish Miracle of PISA: Historical and Sociological Remarks on Teaching and Teacher Education." *Comparative Education*, 41 no. 4, 2005: 455–470.

Simon, Nicole S. and Susan Moore Johnson. (2013). "Teacher Turnover in High Poverty Schools: What We Know and Can Do." From http://isites.harvard.edu/fs/docs/icb.topic1231814.files/Teacher%20Turnover%20in%20High-Poverty%20Schools.pdf

Skiba, Russell J., Robert H. Horner, Choong-Geun Chung, M. Karega Rausch, Seth L. May, and Tary Tobin. "Race is Not Neutral:An Investigation of African American and Latino Disproportionality in School Discipline." *School Psychology Review*, 40 no. 1: 85–107.

Skiba, Russell J. and Kimberly Knesting. "Zero Tolerance, Zero Evidence: An Analysis of School Disciplinary Practice." *New Directions in Youth Development*, 92, 2001: 17–43.

Skiba, Russell J. and Reece L. Peterson. "School Discipline at a Crossroads: From Zero Tolerance to Early Response." *Exceptional Children*, 66 no. 3, 2000: 335–346.

Sleeter, Christine. "Preparing Teachers for Culturally Diverse Schools: Research and the Overwhelming Prsence of Whiteness." *Journal of Teacher Education*, 52 no. 2, 94–106.

Solochek, Jeffrey S. (October 1, 2013). "Teachers Were Not Involved in the Common Core State Standards, Say Common Core Opponents." From http://www. politifact.com/florida/statements/2013/oct/21/public-comments-common-core-hearing/teachers-were-not-involved-developing-common-core-/

Starkey, Louise, Anne Yates, Luanna H. Meyer, Cedric Hall, Mike Taylor, Susan Stevens, and Rawiri Toia. "Professional Development Design: Embedding Educationl reform in New Zealand." *Teaching and Teacher Education*, 25, 2009: 181–189.

Stein, Nancy. "The Gang Truce: A Movement for Social Justice." *Social Justice*, 12 no. 1, 1997. From https://www.questia.com/library/journal/1G1-20562421/the-gang-truce-a-movement-for-social-justice

Strauss, Valerie. (August 7, 2012). "The Big Business of Charter Schools." *The Washington Post*. From http://www.washingtonpost.com/blogs/answer-sheet/post/the-big-business-of-charter-schols/2012/08/16/bdafeca-e7ff-11e1-8487-64e4b2a79ba8_blog.html

Texas Freedom Network. From http://tfn.org/issue/education

Timar, Thomas B. and Julia Maxwell-Jolly. *Narrowing the Achievement Gap*. Cambridge, MA: Harvard Education Press, 2012.

Toom, Auli, Heikki Kynaslahti, Leena Krokfors, Ritta Jyrhama, Reijo Byman, Katarina Stenberg, Katrilna Maaranen, and Pertti Kansanen. "Experiences of a Research-based Approach to Teacher Education: Suggestions and Future Policies." *European Journal of Education*, 45 no. 2, 2010: 331–344.

Tonry, Michael. "Rethinking Unthinkable Punishment Policies in America." *UCLA Law Review*, 46 no. 4, 1999: 1751–1991.

Tyack, David and Larry Cuban. *Tinkering Toward Utopia*. Cambridge, MA: Harvard University Press, 1995.

Vallijarvi, Jouni, Pirjo Linnakyla, Pekka Kupari, Pasi Reinikainen, and Inga Arffman. "Finnish Success in PISA—And Some Reasons Behind It: PISA 2000." Jyvaskyla: Institue for Educational Research, University of Jyvaskyla. From http://eric. ed.gov/?id=ED478054

Van Maele, Dimitri and Mieke Van Houtte. "The Quality of School Life: Teacher-Student Trust Relationships and the Organizational School Context." *Social Indicators Research*, 100, 2011: 85–100.

Varghese, N.V. "Decentralisation of Educational Planning in India: The Case of the District Primary Education Programme." *International Journal of Educational Development*, 16 no. 4, 1996: 355–365.

Villegas, Ana Maria and Tamara Lucas. "Preparing Culturally Responsive Teachers: Rethinking the Curriculum." *Journal of Teacher Education*, 53 no. 1, 2002: 20–32.

von der Embse, Nathaniel, Justin Barterian, and Natasha Segool. "Test Anxiety Interventions for Children and Adolescents: A Systematic Review of Treatment Studies from 2000–2010." *Psychology in the Schools*, 50 no. 1, 2013: 57–71.

Warren, Mark. R. "Communities and Schools: A New View of Urban Education Reform." *Harvard Educational Review*, 75 no. 2, 2001: 133–173.

Warren, Mark R. Soo Hong, Carolyn Leung Rubin, and Phitsamay Suchitkokong Uy. "Beyond the Bake Sale: A Community-Based Relational Approach to Parent Engagement in Schools." *Teachers College Record*, 111 no. 9, 2009: 2209–2254.

Weinstein, Carol, Mary Curran, and Saundra Tomlinson-Clarke. "Culturally Responsive Classroom Management." *Theory Into Practice*, 2 no. 4, 2003: 269–276.

Weissman, Marsha. "Aspiring to the Impracticable: Alternatives to Incarceration in the Era of Mass Incarceration." *NYU Review of Law & Social Change*, 33, 2009: 235–269.

Western, Bruce and Christopher Wildeman. "Punishment, Inequality, and the Future of Mass Incarceration." *Kansas Law Review*, 57, 2009: 852–877.

Wiggin, Addison. (2013). "Charter School Gravy Train Runs Express to Fat City." *Forbes*. From http://www.forbes.com/sites/greatspeculations/2013/09/10/charter-school-gravy-train-runs-express-to-fat-city/#63772f2270e5

Wildeman, Christopher. "Parental Imprisonment, the Prison Boom, and the Concentration of Childhood Disadvantage." *Demography*, 46 no. 2, 2009: 265–280.

Wren, Douglas C. and Jeri Bensen. "Measuring Test Anxiety in Children: Scale Development and Internal Construct Validation." *Anxiety, Stress, and Coping*, 17 no. 3, 2004: 227–240.

Zittel, Thomas and Dieter Fuchs. *Participatory Democracy and Political Participation: Can Participatory Engineering Bring Citizens Back In?* New York: Routledge, 2006.